CREATIVE TEACHING
AND LEARNING

Biographical details

Marilyn Fryer (BA (Hons) PhD GradCertEd CPsychol AFBPsS FRSA), a qualified teacher and chartered psychologist, is director of the Centre for Innovation and Creativity at Leeds Metropolitan University. She teaches cognitive psychology and applied creativity and has introduced creative education into a wide range of degree and diploma courses. She manages the Professional Diploma and Advanced Professional Diploma courses in Applied Creativity. In 1994, Dr Fryer was appointed visiting professor of creativity at the Technical University, Iasi, Romania. She is involved in several international research projects and supervises higher degree students internationally. She is a member of the Creative Education Foundation and the International Creativity Network. She has published in the academic and popular press and has presented refereed papers in Belgium, Germany, Romania and the United States.

Creative Teaching and Learning

Marilyn Fryer

P·C·P
Paul Chapman
Publishing Ltd

Paul Chapman Publishing Ltd
144 Liverpool Road
London
N1 1LA

British Library Cataloguing in Publication Data

Fryer, Marilyn
Creative Teaching and Learning
I.Title
371.102

ISBN 1–85396–256–2

Typeset by Whitelaw & Palmer Ltd, Glasgow
Printed and bound by Athenaeum Press, Gateshead, Tyne & Wear

A B C D E F G H   9 8 7 6

Contents

Preface

Creative Teaching and Learning is for everyone interested in creativity, creative problem solving and innovative teaching and learning. It is especially for teachers who want their students to become efficient learners, skilled in creative thinking and problem solving. This book is also relevant to teacher trainers, trainee teachers, youth and community workers and all those involved in education, training and personal development.

This book reports on what over a thousand experienced teachers and further education lecturers have to say about creativity and how this relates to their work in the classroom. Alongside, there is a summary evaluation of the most relevant literature. An outline of what creative teaching and learning involves is gradually developed and extended to provide a comprehensive picture of this complex subject.

Please note: For ease of reading, the term *teachers* is generally used to denote all the staff (including further education lecturers) whose views are reported in this book. The terms *pupils* and *students* are used interchangeably to denote the under eighteen-year-olds they teach.

Acknowledgements

Many people deserve my thanks. Firstly, I am really grateful to all the 1028 teachers and lecturers who gave so freely of their time, despite so many other pressing demands. Seventy-two children also willingly took part in interviews and many others welcomed me into their classrooms.

Among my colleagues at Leeds Metropolitan University, I owe a special debt of gratitude to Professor John Collings for his guidance throughout the research project and his resilience in the face of innumerable draft reports and mountains of data. Dr Richard Perkin has been a valuable source of advice and encouragement. Efficient library and computing assistance was provided by Max McMurdo, Dr Paul Marchant and their colleagues. Paul Scofield deserves special thanks for his consistent support and enthusiasm.

I would like to thank all my friends and colleagues overseas who have had a considerable effect on my thinking. I wish to single out just five who have made a significant impact on this book. They are Professor E. Paul Torrance, Professor Morris I. Stein, Dr Doris J. Shallcross, Professor Sidney J. Parnes and Dr Edgar Mitchell. I greatly appreciate their support and encouragement.

I must thank my family too. My husband, Barry Fryer, spent many hours discussing ideas with me and checking the drafts. Caroline Fryer helped me decide how best to organize the material and Julia Fryer provided the cartoons portraying what some of the teachers would like to be one day!

Funding from the Economic and Social Research Council and Leeds Metropolitan University made it possible for me to carry out the research reported in this book. I appreciate the friendly co-operation of all concerned.

Finally I should like to thank Paul Chapman Publishing for their help and advice, especially Marianne Lagrange for her extraordinary patience and good humour.

Any errors are my own.

Marilyn Fryer,
July 1995

1

Creativity in teaching and learning

> Creativity is one of the things that distinguishes human beings from animals.
> (head of chemistry)

The capacity to be creative is intensely human. It is essential for survival. It is, therefore, all the more surprising that creativity is generally neglected in mainstream education. This is not the case in business and industry. Large organizations, especially multinational corporations, are spending a lot of money to ensure that their top executives become skilled in creative problem solving. Why? Because they have found such skills help them stay ahead of the field, invent new products and save money.

But schooling is about more than preparing people for work. There are even more fundamental reasons for putting creativity on the educational agenda. These reasons have to do with how we learn, think and solve problems – presumably this *is* what we want children to be able to do.

Hopefully we do, because there has never before been a time when such skills were so in demand. If children and young people are to keep pace with the accelerating rate of technological and social change, then they will all need creative skills – skills which are as basic as reading, writing and adding up.

This book reports on the largest, most comprehensive investigation of its kind – Project 1000. It charts the views of over a thousand British teachers and further education lecturers about creativity in teaching and learning. This investigation involved both a survey and an interview study. The use of both quantitative and qualitative data collection techniques makes it possible to report findings with wide applicability and to illustrate them with teachers' personal accounts. Further details are given in Fryer (1989; 1994b) and Fryer and Collings (1991a; 1991b), apart from some of the qualitative data which is presented for the first time in this book.

The staff involved in this investigation work in a wide variety of circumstances, teaching a diverse array of subjects. Teachers and lecturers working with every age group from five to eighteen years are included. Data have been collected in five major regions of Britain (excluding Scotland), some from schools and the rest from staff undertaking a whole range of in-service courses up and down the country. Some new and surprising findings are revealed. What the teachers think about creativity and how this relates to their preferred way of teaching is set in the context of the most relevant literature to date, on which the author, a qualified teacher, university lecturer and chartered psychologist, offers her own unique perspective.

Teachers play an important role in improving children's capacity to be creative and they can offer valuable insights on teaching and learning, yet their views have rarely been sought. Previously there have been very few comprehensive accounts of teachers' views on creativity. An exception is a Swedish investigation by Bjerstedt (1976). Nor do there appear to have been any previous major investigations which have focused concurrently on teachers' views about creativity and their preferred ways of teaching. These were found to be linked (see Chapter 5).

Activity 1

Take a few moments to think about what comes into your mind when you think of 'creativity' and make some notes.

This is how a headteacher replied:

Creativity is to do with being imaginative and developing ideas that are not totally second-hand. I see it more intellectually, not necessarily doing or making something, maybe because I'm useless at that . . . it's to do with being able to look at a situation or what someone else has said and work on it and take it on.

A primary headteacher commented 'It's extremely hard to define. The people I think are truly creative are those who find uncommon options or solutions or ways of doing things . . . people who come up with a very simple solution to something that's foxed everyone for ages'.

These teachers' descriptions of creativity are applicable to any curriculum area, yet most people would think it odd to talk about the 'creative sciences'. The 'creative arts' sounds a lot more acceptable, even though there is good evidence that the creative process is essentially the same in both the arts and the sciences (see for instance Weisberg, 1993). However, not all teachers see creativity as relevant to all areas of the curriculum. Two-thirds of those involved in Project 1000 thought it was only applicable to certain subjects.

To find out where the teachers think creativity fits into the school curriculum a creativity exhibition was held and schools were invited to loan whatever they thought suitable. In all, two hundred pieces of work were submitted. The results were very telling. Almost all the exhibits comprised art, craft, stories and poems. The exceptions were a song written and recorded by one student, games invented by upper juniors and some graphical work. But that was all. There were no examples of creative work in science. It appears that the schools involved in the exhibition mainly associate creativity with the arts. These results are not entirely surprising. However, less schools took part in the exhibition than in the whole survey (Fryer, 1989). In the study as a whole, the majority of teachers (68 per cent) who recalled creativity development being included in their training said this was in the arts. Hardly any recalled its inclusion in maths, science and technology (4 per cent) or in business studies (0.7 per cent).

Yet some teachers do acknowledge the wider relevance of creativity, for example:

In technology, a pupil who can pick a problem and find a solution is more useful than someone who can simply pass a physics exam. I've come from industry. I think that's what we want – people who can actually see their way round a problem and come up with solutions. We don't give that much credence in Britain. The people who get the credit are the money makers and the manipulators. Those who are coming up with decent solutions to society's problems are not making any money. We need to do an awful lot more to recognize creativity and give it some credence. Seeing a problem and finding an answer, that's creativity.

(technology teacher)

If children don't have any original ideas, I think they're just role-playing. There are plenty of intelligent people around, learning facts and with good memories, but in both science and the arts you've got to be creative. In science, design, architecture and in the classroom, you've got to be original. I think creativity is very important.

(infant teacher)

Later on, we shall be examining the role of creativity in the classroom in some depth, but first let us review some of the arguments which have been put forward in favour of including creativity on the educational agenda. These arguments relate to three levels of human activity – individual, societal and global.

INDIVIDUAL QUALITY OF LIFE

The structure of work is changing. The amount of paid employment available seems to be diminishing, despite the fact that there is no shortage of work to be done. Young people with a creative approach to living will be in a better position to take advantage of opportunities and create their own employment. The ability to be creative in an artistic sense can also be a source of personal satisfaction, as a primary headmaster remarked, 'The system of education in secondary/higher education demands the abandonment of artistic subjects for the majority of pupils. Options are often made with a view to preparing for a job. Art and craft need to be encouraged for all pupils as a means of self-satisfaction'.

Warnock (1976, p. 203) has argued that 'it is the main purpose of education to give people the opportunity of not ever being . . . bored'. Yet at present in the UK, there is evidence that many children do find school boring. For example, Barber (1994, p. 2) has found that 70 per cent of British high school students 'count the minutes to the end of their lessons'. He also reports that 'Thirty per cent believe that work is boring and 30–40 per cent . . . would rather not go to school'.

One way of overcoming school boredom is to give students the opportunity of employing creative and innovative skills on real-life problems. Such learning is likely to be exciting and challenging. Students who enjoy learning are more inclined to be effective learners, so teaching also becomes more rewarding. A high school chemistry teacher recounted how he captures the imagination of his students, some of whom are quite switched off by other lessons:

> I find some of the really difficult children, who might otherwise be away, turn up for science. It's noisy and their notebooks are not wonderfully kept, but in terms of enjoyment and participation it's good. I don't think you can be creative unless you involve yourself and are enjoying yourself.

Further details of his approach to teaching are given in Chapter 7.

Artistic creativity also has a therapeutic value, something which is appreciated by an FE art and design lecturer working with young people of low self-esteem. Many of her students arrive in her class with such a low opinion of themselves that, at first, they find it really difficult to cope with being praised. One student felt so inadequate that he regularly took sanctuary under the table. Here is what she has to say:

> I think being in touch with one's creativity is important for mental health. Being able to be creative does create peace and I think there's nothing better at the end of the day than feeling that you've achieved something. Students sometimes say they feel they've done something good and it has an important effect on them as people. There's no doubt that art and craft is therapeutic in mental illness. It's funny how all of a sudden, when the ordinary day-to-day workings of the brain break down or someone goes against society and commits a crime, that they're given something creative to do to set them going again. It's interesting that all of a sudden it becomes important, whereas it's not thought important when people are in general education.

The arts are also seen as a means of helping everyone, regardless of their specialism, to develop their creative thinking skills. A primary headteacher was 'greatly concerned about the emphasis on maths and science and the inappropriate neglect of the arts, an area in which people . . . are allowed freedom of expression and learn to think differently. Such neglect will ultimately be to science's and society's cost'.

SOCIETAL AND GLOBAL ISSUES

Most social structures, including political systems, have evolved slowly over the centuries, but many of them are no longer appropriate to the modern world. People will need to be both flexible and resourceful if they are to adjust to the 'rapid multidimensional transformation of social, political, economic, demographic and cultural aspects of life' and increasing globalization (Ayman, 1993). At the 1993 President's Convocation of the Creative Education Foundation, USA, Dr Iraj Ayman stressed the key role that education has to play in enabling young people to deal with this transformation effectively and in ethically sound ways.

Those responsible for future policy will need to be skilled in making difficult decisions both wisely and quickly. This may seem far removed from the everyday life of the classroom, but people who can make such decisions may soon be in short supply, unless we educate for the future now.

Of course, not everyone will be called upon to make far-reaching decisions, but we all need to be able to make socially responsible choices. As our lives become more complex, we need to be increasingly skilled in recognizing and weighing up alternative courses of action. It is skills like these which training in creative problem solving is designed to foster. Such training can have another valuable social function, which is to help us see things from differing perspectives. The ability to appreciate other people's points of view is especially valuable in times of social upheaval. Even more crucial is young people's ability to think for themselves, to avoid falling prey to external forms of control (Ayman, 1993).

At the same convocation, the astronaut Dr Edgar Mitchell, famous for his moon-walk, voiced his concern about the accelerating rate of change on a global scale (see Figures 1.1 and 1.2). The explosion of new knowledge is now so great that most of the things that young children are currently learning will be obsolete by the time they grow up. We have never been in this situation before.

Mitchell is really concerned that, because of the exponential way in which major global changes are occurring, it is possible to be entirely oblivious of what is happening to the planet, until it is virtually too late to do anything about it. To illustrate his point, he uses the simple analogy of weed covering a pond (Figure 1.3). The diagram shows how the weed problem does not become really obvious until the twenty-eighth day – only two days before the pond becomes entirely smothered. In other words, by the time we are sure that some kind of intervention is necessary, there is very little time to act and very little margin for error (Mitchell, 1993).

Training in creative problem solving can enable people to be skilled in finding the best solution quickly in these kinds of situations (see for instance Parnes, 1992a). Most school curricula comprise received knowledge from the past but offer woefully inadequate preparation for the future (Guilford, 1977; De Bono, 1993).

To cope with the demands of the future, people will have to be quick-thinking, flexible and imaginative. They will need to be competent in producing effective solutions to unfamiliar problems in unclear situations. If creativity development were to have the same status in education as it does in the corporate setting, then children would be in a much better position to cope with these kinds of challenges.

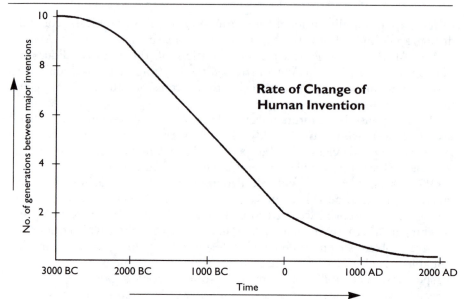

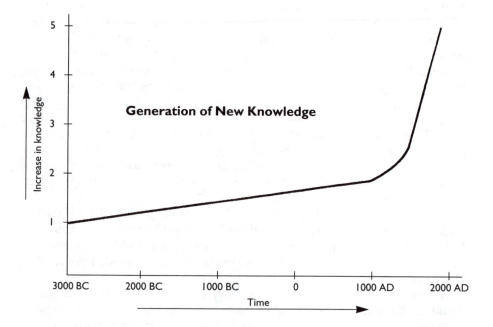

Figure 1.1   The increasing pace of change: two examples (reproduced with the kind permission of Dr Edgar Mitchell)

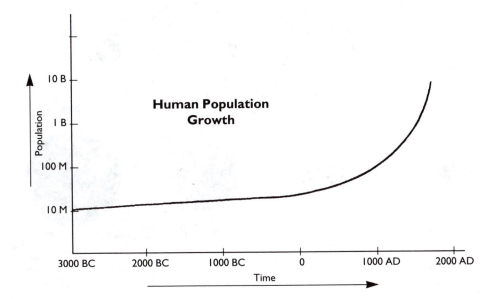

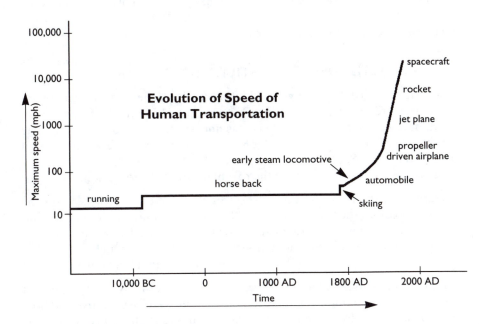

Figure 1.2 Change in a shrinking world: two examples (reproduced with the kind permission of Dr Edgar Mitchell)

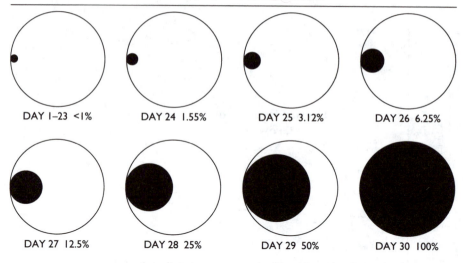

DAY 1–23 <1%   DAY 24 1.55%   DAY 25 3.12%   DAY 26 6.25%

DAY 27 12.5%   DAY 28 25%   DAY 29 50%   DAY 30 100%

Figure 1.3 Exponential growth in a limited space (reproduced with the kind permission of Dr Edgar Mitchell)

This kind of argument is not new. Since the 1960s, Dr Paul Torrance has been urging educators to equip children and young people with the skills to solve the problems we cannot yet imagine. Indeed, Torrance's personal contribution to this field has been remarkable. But now there is a new dimension – the accelerating rate of change.

ATTITUDES TO CREATIVITY IN EDUCATION

All but one of the 1028 staff involved in Project 1000 believe that creativity has some role in teaching and learning. 17 per cent (176) think it has a very important role; 9 per cent (94) believe it is not especially important, whilst the majority of teachers 74 per cent (758) rate it somewhere between the two extremes (Fryer, 1989; Fryer and Collings, 1991a).

Here is how some staff describe the role of creativity in education:

Creativity is the most desirable aspect of the task of the teacher and the school, possibly the most important. It is needing much more debate and teachers need more techniques to encourage it. I feel I have not thought about it enough and been able to translate that into my practice.

(high school humanities teacher)

I find this area fascinating. It's not something I think of day to day. It would interest me to find out from other staff when they were last creative and how they defined it. I don't think there's enough emphasis on creativity, not just in professional life, but in our private lives too.

(high school teacher-librarian)

Creativity is important, but no more important than other aspects of a child's development. It is simply one of the facets of developing a child's character. Children should be encouraged to be creative and to enjoy it, so that they can become whole individuals enjoying life to the full. Creativity contributes to both the child's academic and social development.

(year head, juniors)

An inner-city primary teacher saw creativity as 'absolutely crucial. Children learn more quickly and more effectively if they are required to think creatively, than simply respond to a mechanical task'.

An English and drama teacher commented 'I'm glad someone's looking at creativity and realizing it's a vital part of children's development, because I think children are losing out drastically now. There's a part of a child's life that's being missed somewhere'.

A science teacher, working in an inner-city junior school, thought that developing creativity was important because 'ultimately children will have to think for themselves'. She was worried, however, that she might be doing her pupils a disservice in getting them to think for themselves, since this might make them reject the type of 'cramming teaching' she thought happened in high schools in preparation for national examinations. Nevertheless, she liked teaching in this way as she enjoyed the variety involved. A junior school geography teacher, also working in the inner city, declared 'If you don't want creativity, you don't want a teacher'.

Developing creative thinking skills is so often neglected in education yet children can get practice in creative thinking by tackling suitably designed tasks in any curriculum area. What creative problem solving demands is the pupil's commitment to the task. Real involvement in learning usually leads to a deeper understanding (see for instance Entwistle, 1982) and what pupils understand they remember (Craik and Lockhart, 1972). This is not to suggest that other ways of teaching and learning need to be abandoned. It is more often a case of supplementing rather than replacing. The aim is to redress the balance, not to tip it in the opposite direction.

Later we will examine *creative thinking* and *creativity development*. We will delve into issues which are hotly debated such as how transferable are creative skills from one subject area to another. Does it even make sense to talk about creative skills? . . . and so on. But first we examine the concept of creativity more closely.

 Activity 2
Based on what you have read so far, write your own definition of creativity.

DEFINING CREATIVITY

The teachers who took part in the interview study were also asked for their immediate definitions of creativity (Fryer, 1989). This kind of approach which requires a 'snap answer' to a question may well reveal what people really think, because it is 'less open to defensive bias and face-saving' than a more considered response would be, as discussed by Oppenheim (1966, p. 77). Here is how several teachers responded:

Creativity is being original, being able to take an idea forward and develop it in your own way.

(primary teacher)

For most people creativity is a subconscious process.

(lecturer in construction)

Creativity is what one person produces and is interested in. Anyone can be creative, but not everyone is.

(lecturer in electronics)

I see creativity as ideas basically. These can be translated into various areas. Creativity involves first of all thinking, imagining. If you can get a child to think or imagine, whether it's art, craft, music or poetry. Get children to think for themselves. That's one of our biggest aims. Creativity is not something that can be superimposed.

(primary teacher)

Creativity seems to have been largely applied to products, but the creative manipulation of ideas is of great significance – advertising, religion, personal relationships, even teaching.

(head of design)

With the arts at least, creativity is so wide and spread out that giving it a definition is in fact giving false restrictions to something that should have no restriction at all.

(head of art)

Creativity is the ability to look at things in a different way, to find satisfaction in making or creating something and persevering with it until the end-product. It involves hard work. It's not airy-fairy.

(primary head)

I don't know if I can define it. It's something about breaking ground. I don't think it can be defined absolutely because what is creative for one person might be run-of-the-mill for another. It's something to do with enlightenment and making connections – obvious and non-obvious. It's about discovery. I don't think there needs to be an end-product. Creativity doesn't often get tapped by the teacher.

(teacher-librarian)

It's putting an idea forward. Often the first idea that comes to mind is a cliché. You have to keep pushing beyond that and being disciplined. It's only by experimenting and doodling and making trial runs that other things become apparent. At the starting point you can't realize what the final objective is going to be. It's a series of investigative steps, comparisons and happy accidents. Creativity is about self-awareness. You can't rely on others to tell you what's wrong or right. You can to begin with, but eventually it's got to be your own decision. I think it's a very personal thing, creativity. You have an awareness yourself. People will express it in different ways from others. Perhaps to the lay-person it's not always recognizable.

(art and photography high school teacher)

These responses raise a few more issues such as: How original does something have to be to count as creative? How helpful are notions like 'the subconscious' in describing the creative process? Does there have to be a tangible end-product or does an idea count as creative? Who can decide what counts? What kinds of environments are most conducive to the development of creativity? These are the kinds of issues we shall address.

Creativity has a reputation for being a notoriously difficult concept to pin down, even though it is no more difficult to get to grips with than other concepts we find easier to accept such as love, learning or education (Holloway, 1978). Holloway describes such concepts as *fuzzy*, because not all of their distinguishing features are evident in every instance, as in Chinese writing. In the case of creativity, it is possible to focus on either the person creating, the created product or idea, the process of being creative or the environment in which this occurs – or indeed any combination of these, as illustrated by the following examples:

Process

Creative activity appears simply to be a special class of problem solving activity characterized by novelty.

(Newell, Shaw and Simon)

Product

Creativity is the occurrence of a composition which is both new and valuable.

(Henry A. Murray)

Person

Creativity is the disposition to make and to recognize valuable innovations.

(H. D. Lasswell)

Creativity is the ability to *see* (or be aware) and to *respond*.

(Erich Fromm, original emphasis)

Environment

The reciprocal relationship between culture and creativity is such that a creative product is not really an invention unless it is socially accepted. The creative product has to operate within the culture; it has to work. If it does not work, it is a failure as an invention.

(Morton I. Teicher)
(*Source*: Fabun, 1968, pp. 3, 4, 26)

It would be artificial to envisage any of the four categories (person, product, process or environment) as independent of the rest. They all interact – something which is better reflected in the following more comprehensive definitions:

The creative process . . . is the emergence in action of a novel relational product, growing out of the uniqueness of the individual on the one hand, and the materials, events, people, or circumstances of his life on the other.

(Rogers, 1954, quoted in Vernon, 1970, p. 139)

Creativity is a process that results in novelty which is accepted as useful, tenable, or satisfying by a significant group of others at some point in time.

(Stein, 1984, p. 1)

One of the strengths of Stein's definition is that it allows for a sociocultural dimension – a dynamic relationship between individuals and their environment. Stein also points out that, although education normally emphasizes the cognitive, motivational and emotional factors are just as relevant. For a complete understanding of creativity, it is necessary to take account of them all (Stein, 1994c).

Table 1.1 shows those aspects of creativity with which the teachers as a group most identify. From this it can be seen that the most popular way of envisaging creativity is in terms of imagination, with originality coming a close second:

I see creativity as the ability to imagine and put imagination into effect.

(FE lecturer)

I think it's about producing something highly personal. You might want to use others' ideas, but what you produce at the end of the day is your individual product. It's also being given the space, the opportunity, to be original in a mental sense.

(FE Social Care lecturer)

Alex Osborn, founder of the Creative Education Foundation, regards the ability to imagine as central to the concept of creativity (Osborn, 1993). However, in the literature as a whole, it is divergent thinking i.e. generating a range of ideas, which is most emphasized (Hocevar, 1981).

According to Guilford (1977) and Parnes (1992a), creativity also involves convergence, as when homing in on an appropriate solution. Yet only 10 per cent of the teachers see this as integral to the creative process. Their response is not really surprising since popular notions of creativity stress idea generation

Table 1.1 Perceptions of creativity among Project 1000 teachers (N = 1028)

Aspect	%
Imagination	88.7
Original ideas	80.1
Self-expression	73.7
Discovery	65.4
Seeing connections	65.4
Invention	61.4
Innovation	59.3
Divergent thinking	53.8
Thinking processes	51.9
Awareness of beauty	49.7
Combining ideas	49.5
Inspiration	46.6
Aesthetic products	33.6
Valuable ideas	32.8
Unconscious activities	18.1
Convergent thinking	10.2
Mysterious processes	9.8
Tangible products	9.5
Other aspects	5.0

Source: Fryer, 1989.

more than the selection of a suitable solution. The creative process is discussed more fully in Chapter 4, where alternative terminology is suggested.

MODERN AND TRADITIONAL PERCEPTIONS OF CREATIVITY

The teachers involved in Project 1000 have a modern view of creativity insofar as hardly any of them see it as mysterious or involving notions of an *unconscious*. Yet, nearly half of them think inspiration is involved. The notion of inspiration can be traced back to the Ancient World (Weisberg, 1993; see also Chapter 4).

What is really surprising is that 70 per cent of the teachers believe creativity is a rare gift. This contrasts quite sharply with the American view. In the United States creativity has been perceived as amenable to development in most individuals since the Second World War (Razik, 1967). But apart from its association with the arts, creative education in Britain tends to be most commonly associated with giftedness. The term *gift* seems to imply some kind of finite innate ability, a view which is difficult to defend psychologically. Nor is it especially accurate, since many advocates of gifted programmes, such as Treffinger, see these as useful for all pupils. Substitution of the term *excellence*, as recommended by Stein (1994c), would counter an awful lot of faulty perception, confusion and misguided élitism.

Opinions differ about what level of achievement may legitimately be regarded as creative. One source of confusion is that the terms *creative* and *creativity* have been used freely – far too freely in Stein's view. He points out that they have been used for 'paradigmatic shifts (Kuhn, 1970), big and little inventions, "new and improved" products, creative cookery . . . and for creative financing (usually for "questionable" deals)' (Stein, 1983, p. 1).

Some argue that only high level achievements, such as great works of art, can be legitimately called creative (see for instance Ausubel, 1978). It is, therefore, hardly surprising that those who hold this view regard creativity as something which only geniuses have. Others maintain that we all have the capacity to be creative, but in varying amounts (see for instance Weisberg, 1993).

The head of an inner London comprehensive high school explained why she sees creativity as rare:

> Often a lot of what you read is a re-hash of what someone else has written. I'm a historian and [most people are] part of a system . . . and then you're a cog in a wheel, processing received information. When I said it was rare, I meant very few people seem to have the ability and opportunity to get out of that and stand back and stop and can really say, 'That was me; that was original' . . . maybe it's the opportunity that's rare, rather than the ability.

One of this head teacher's highest priorities is to help her students realize that opportunities do exist. She and her staff achieve this partly by helping to raise the pupils' self-esteem, but also by heightening their awareness of opportunities which they previously did not consider as within their grasp. She has also taken practical steps to improve their learning environment (see Chapter 10).

MALE AND FEMALE PERCEPTIONS OF CREATIVITY

One of the most unexpected findings was the discovery of a marked difference in the way male and female teachers perceive creativity – something which does not appear to have been reported before. The female teachers as a group see creativity in much more personal terms than the male teachers do. When some of the female staff interviewed talked about creativity, many of them referred to it as if it were synonymous with self-expression, for example:

> It's the ability of a person to express himself [or herself] in as many forms as possible, using all sorts of media.
>
> (junior year head, female)

> In a school sense, it's producing for an outsider what is inside you . . . it might be a piece of written work, art work, drama. It's bringing out the inside you to put on show.
>
> (junior teacher, female)

> To be creative means to develop something very personal to yourself.
>
> (primary school teacher, female)

On the whole, male teachers do not perceive creativity in this way. They tend to see it more impersonally. There are other intergroup differences in views about creativity (Fryer and Collings, 1991a) (see also Chapter 5) but it is the differences in male/female views which are most marked. As we shall see in Chapter 2, this also affects how they rate their pupils' work for creativity.

EXPLANATIONS OF CREATIVITY AND THE LEARNING PROCESS

Although imagination is the aspect of creativity with which most teachers identify, many staff have also described creativity as a thinking or problem solving activity.

The literature has also described creativity either in terms of problem solving or imagination. It will be argued in Chapter 4 that these conceptions are not mutually exclusive, but rather provide different levels of explanation.

Debates about the nature of creative thinking (that is, thinking which results in creative ideas) will be dealt with later in the book, but it is worth mentioning here that creative problem solving is widely regarded as most applicable to puzzling, unclear situations or for venturing into uncharted territory. What is not generally mentioned in the creativity literature is that problem solving is far more pervasive in both thinking and learning than is generally acknowledged. In learning, it tends to comprise what is generally referred to as active learning and in thinking, it may be referred to as reasoning. So, we can think of problem solving as linking learning and thinking (see for instance Holloway, 1978). Another connection between learning and thinking is imagination, which in turn is closely associated with creativity, as discussed in Chapter 4 (and in Fryer, 1989; 1994a; building on the work of Johnson-Laird, 1987).

We can also regard memory and perception as link-pins between learning and thinking. This is beginning to sound like an argument for abandoning terms like learning and thinking in favour of the more accurate descriptor, cognition – in other words, reversing the traditional practice of artificially breaking down complex concepts like cognition and creativity into various categories in an attempt to understand them better. Such a strategy has been both helpful and counter-productive. However, it is worth bearing in mind that such categorization is merely a device. In these and other fields, old atomistic approaches are now giving way to more holistic ones, in which the dynamic and complex nature of concepts like creativity and cognition is being recognized.

SUMMARY

The capacity to be creative is closely bound up with what it means to be human. It affects personal well-being and quality of life; it affects how we cope with the quickening pace of social, economic and technological change. Creative skills are in demand as never before. Major organizations who invest in creativity development are finding that it makes a significant difference to their efficiency, effectiveness and hence their success. Paradoxically, such training is largely neglected in mainstream education. Yet there are fundamental reasons why creativity should be on the educational agenda. These reasons have to do with how we learn, think and solve problems.

Teachers can offer valuable insights into teaching and learning. They have a major contribution to make to the development of creative skills, but their views have not been sought as much as might be expected. Those staff who regard the development of creativity as important do so because they realize that ultimately children will have to think for themselves. Three-quarters of those involved in Project 1000 regard creativity as a rare gift, which is quite an old-fashioned view. However, nearly all of them see it as something which can be developed.

Creativity is often regarded as a difficult concept to handle, but really it is no more difficult than concepts like *work* and *play*, *education* even, which we normally find much more acceptable. A common way of making creativity a more manageable concept to deal with is to focus on the creative process, person, product or idea, the environment or any combination of these.

The investigation described in this book offers clear evidence that male and female teachers perceive creativity in quite different terms, with female staff envisaging it in much more personal terms than the male staff.

2

Assessing creativity

In God we trust. All others must have data.

(anon. quoted in Stein, 1984, p. 44)

This chapter reveals how the teachers prefer to assess their students' creativity and the criteria they value. The criteria they choose provides yet another insight into how they see creativity.

 Activity 3

Before reading this chapter, think of something you regard as creative. This could be a work of art, a piece of work, a good idea, an interesting lesson or the way an organization or school is run. Think about how you would evaluate the creative merit of whatever you have selected. What criteria have you chosen?.

WHAT TO ASSESS

Various sources of data can be used as the basis for evaluating pupils' creativity. Teachers can monitor what their pupils have to say; observe their behaviour; examine the work they produce; administer creativity tests or use any combination of these and other approaches. To get a complete picture of an individual's capabilities, it is also a good idea to gather data from people who know the learner well and be willing to reassess from time to time (Stein, 1993).

According to Hocevar (1981, p. 459) one of the most reliable indicators of creativity is 'a simple and straightforward inventory of creative achievement and activities'. In keeping with good practice, the teachers involved in Project 1000 prefer to collect data on their students' creative performance from a number of sources. Almost all of them (95 per cent) really value their students' ideas and questions; the work produced is next most popular (82 per cent), with students' behaviour a close third (72 per cent). Less than five per cent of teachers are keen on testing.

One reason for their reluctance to use tests may relate to a suspicion of formal testing in general. Interestingly, the Torrance Tests of Creative Thinking – probably the best-known creativity tests – have been found to be good at predicting creative achievement in later life (Torrance, 1974). The evidence suggests that British teachers, on the whole, have very little experience of creativity tests.

The teachers voiced strong objections to externally imposed testing *per se*, since they regard it as merely duplicating their normal practice of continually monitoring children's progress. What they most fear is that education will degenerate into rote learning, with staff reduced to merely 'teaching to a test'. As a London primary teacher pointed out, 'there are ways of heightening children's test performance which are not educationally sound in the long run'.

Ideas or products

There is some disagreement about whether an idea *per se* can count as creative or whether there has to be a tangible product. On the one hand, there is an argument that it is difficult to gauge the level of creativity when there is no tangible product. On the other hand, it is hard to argue that good ideas and plans are not admissible, simply because they have not been translated into reality. School and college work often falls into the ideas category – albeit 'ideas on paper'. However, as a head of design working in Devon pointed out, architects' plans and designers' projects also comprise ideas on paper. The fact that they may not have been translated into tangible products surely does not make them any less creative.

Reality, fantasy and artistic creativity

Sometimes creativity is erroneously associated with fantasy. However, citing the playwright, Edward Bond, Best (1982, p. 289, original emphasis) points out that this is inaccurate:

> It is commonly believed that to insist that imagination is central to the arts is to say that the arts are concerned with phantasies, illusions, escape from reality. In fact, imagination is required in art in order to peel away the illusions and see the truth . . . . The creative vision or imagination of the artist is required not simply to escape from *reality*, but also to escape from the *romantic illusions* which preclude a truthful conception of reality.

A high school English teacher appeared to be thinking along the same lines when he remarked that he would rather children wrote effectively about what they knew, than produced a fantasy about which they had no knowledge.

EXTERNAL INFLUENCES

Students' grades are often regarded as only indicative of their ability, as if the teachers' skills, the learning context and so on had no effect, as one teacher pointed out:

As a teacher, I'm very conscious that, when we assess students, all too often we do this as if they were in some kind of vacuum. There has to be something pretty unusual affecting the results before we like to acknowledge that it's more than their achievement that's being assessed. I know marks can be moderated and teaching quality monitored and so forth, but they're still part of an interactive system. All too often grades are taken as absolute indicators of capability. It's a sobering experience to think just how much teachers' evaluations are taken to heart by their students.

It is impossible to disentangle the production of creative work and its evaluation from contextual influences (see for instance Stein, 1984), but this phenomenon is not restricted to creativity. It applies just as much to other concepts – wealth, happiness and health, for example. What it means for creativity is that there can never be any 'definitive' criteria. Fortunately, this does not mean there are no relevant ones.

ASSESSMENT CRITERIA

The teachers' preferred criteria

It can be quite puzzling to know how to go about assessing creativity, as illustrated by the following teacher's externalized thinking:

> Is it just a good example of something normal or is it creative? The only way I can say it's creative depends. [pause] If you know what's gone into it, that's the starting point. Kids have got the most amazing internal gauge for themselves about whether their work is OK or whether it means anything to them . . . I don't know.

When the whole group of teachers were asked what criteria they preferred for judging the creativity of students' work, the most popular ones turned out to be 'imaginative' and 'original' (see Table 2.1). In an interview, an electronics lecturer, who was himself prolifically creative, said he wanted his students' work to be 'fresh'.

'Showing initiative', 'pleasing to the pupil' and 'expressing depth of feeling' are almost as popular with the teachers as a whole, but less than a quarter of them envisage 'appropriate' as relevant. Only just over a tenth identify with 'useful' and a twentieth with 'elegant'. This matters. Products and ideas which are just 'original' may have little or no merit. They could be simply bizarre. Various investigators have come to the conclusion that to justify the description 'creative', work must be not only original but also appropriate, useful and valuable. The elegance of a solution is much valued in science, mathematics and design. It is also highly regarded in creative problem solving activities such as Synectics (see for instance Gordon, 1961).

Table 2.1   Preferred criteria for assessing creativity among Project 1000 teachers (N = 1028)

Criteria	%
Imaginative	87.5
Original for the pupil	84.7
Showing initiative	79.9
Pleasing to the pupil	74.0
Expressing depth of feeling	70.3
Expressing an independent viewpoint	66.7
Demonstrating depth of thinking	64.9
Demonstrating idea progression	64.4
Qualitatively better than own previous work	63.3
Reflecting child's experiences	47.4
Using appropriate skills	44.5
Element of surprise	42.9
Using appropriate media	38.2
Unique	37.3
Pleasing to the teacher	34.7
Qualitatively better than would be expected from a child of that age	34.7
Pleasing to classmates	29.9
Attractive	26.7
Appropriate	23.4
Qualitatively better than peer performance	23.4
Useful	13.8
Complex	8.4
Accurate	6.8
Elegant	5.7
Other	1.6

Source: Fryer, 1989.

Different groups emphasize different criteria

In keeping with the way they define creativity (see Chapter 1), male and female teachers differ significantly in their approach to creativity assessment. The women teachers put more emphasis on personal factors. For example, they look to see if pupils' work shows depth of feeling or depth of thought. The men, on the other hand, attach more importance to elegance.

When we consider how those teaching different subjects assess work for creativity, the same pattern of responses described in Chapter 1 is evident. Compared with those teaching maths, science or technology, every other subject group is significantly more inclined to look for 'self-expression' criteria as evidence of creativity. When analyses controlling for gender were conducted, significant differences were still evident. At the same time it is important to remember that, within each group, there are individuals whose opinions differ from the group as a whole. These findings appear to be new. A possible explanation is offered in Chapter 5.

How many criteria did you identify in Activity 3? Could they apply equally to both ideas and tangible products?

Besemer and Treffinger's review of criteria

In a review of publications, Besemer and Treffinger (1981, p. 164) identified over one hundred and twenty-five separate criteria, although they acknowledge that they are not all relevant in every instance. Fortunately, they were able to categorize them into just three groups:

- novelty;
- resolution;
- elaboration and synthesis.

Novelty

In their novelty category Besemer and Treffinger include criteria relating to the newness of a product in terms of processes, techniques, concepts and so on. They also include criteria relating to a product's capacity to suggest additional creative products – as when the first painting of a new style suggests a lot of other works in that style. They also include the criterion 'transformational', as identified by Jackson and Messick (1965) as well (see below).

Resolution

Resolution refers to the extent to which a 'product fits, or meets the needs of, a problematic situation'. So it would be judged for adequacy, appropriateness, logic, usefulness and value.

Elaboration and synthesis

Elaboration and synthesis relate to the extent to which a product 'combines unlike elements into a . . . coherent whole'. So this category includes criteria such as – attractiveness, complexity, elegance, expressiveness, wholeness or completeness and the extent to which it is well-crafted.

Jackson and Messick's four criteria of creativity

Jackson and Messick (1965) identify four criteria for evaluating creative products. They are similar to Besemer and Treffinger's categories and are:

- novelty;
- transformation;
- condensation;
- appropriateness.

Jackson and Messick argue that for a product to be regarded as creative in the highest sense it must satisfy all the criteria.

They define novelty as unusualness. Transformation involves a radical shift in approach. For Jackson and Messick, appropriateness is the extent to which a product is appropriate to its context. Appropriateness is also stressed by Best (1982). He argues that simply being divergent or different is not necessarily creative, but being divergent or different in a way that is appropriate is more likely to be.

Jackson and Messick describe condensation as the capacity to allow continued contemplation without exhausting meanings and implications. This is a very stringent criterion, which only great works are likely to satisfy (Webberley and Litt, 1976). Varnedoe, Director of Painting and Sculpture at the Museum of Modern Art, New York City, makes the related observation that successful art 'detonates a series of possibilities' (Shekerjian, 1991, p. 56). To be accepted it must mean different things to different people and create different and often conflicting agenda.

Other useful criteria are 'effectiveness', suggested by Bruner (1962) and 'relevance', proposed by Kneller (1965). Kneller uses this term to describe the compelling quality of creative products – a quality which makes the observer think 'Why didn't I think of that?'.

All the criteria described above can apply equally to both tangible products and ideas.

APPLYING CREATIVITY CRITERIA

Having identified appropriate assessment criteria, the next step is to decide how to apply them. No-one would expect young people to fulfil all the creativity criteria mentioned above, but they might go some way towards fulfilling some of them. So their work might be judged for 'appropriateness' in terms of the task and their level of development. It is common practice to assess 'novelty' in terms of whether the work is new for that child and so on (Webberley and Litt, 1976).

In their reference to 'originality', Besemer and Treffinger illustrate the difficulty involved in applying creativity criteria – in what sense and to what extent does a product have to be original to count as creative? Many of the Project 1000 teachers said they preferred to judge a child's work against his or her past performance, asking 'Is this piece of work creative for this child?' Attempting to better one's past performance can be really motivating (Bruner, 1966). Gordon (1961, p. 12) has a neat way of assessing 'elegance'. For him, the most elegant solution to a problem is the one which is 'the simplest in proportion to the complexity of the variables involved'.

CONFIDENCE IN CREATIVITY ASSESSMENT

Perhaps not surprisingly, it is the art and design staff who are most confident about assessing creativity. Le Corbusier's sentiments (see for instance Le Corbusier, 1946) are echoed in this example:

Creativity responds to a need. Designs we eventually grow to love, respond to and feel in harmony with are those with a high degree of functional success . . . success for the designer is in terms of the response evoked from the looker/listener.

(Welsh design teacher)

This comment hints at the transactional relationship between creators and appreciators to which Stein has drawn attention. Stein points out that we are all involved in creativity either by being creative or appreciating creativity. To reflect this relationship, he coined the word 'contripication' – a combination of 'contribution' and 'participation' (Stein, 1981).

During a follow-up interview, the teacher quoted above expanded on his ideas with practical examples:

> I firmly believe that if you design a functional chair, which the longer you use it, the more you feel at home in it – the more it becomes a favourite chair, the more the shape delights your eye . . . . If you take two chairs to extremes (I did this once) – a chair with long legs and a high back and compare it with one which supports your thighs and wraps around you, then I would say that in most people's eyes the comfortable chair would be the more harmonious, the more pleasant to look at and the uncomfortable chair would look rather bizarre.
>
> So design has to be functional. The first thoughts you must have when creating or designing are a) What material am I going to use? b) What kind of shapes can I make with it? If you do all these things successfully, it gets degrees more beautiful as you progress. So one concept of beauty might be – 'as near to perfection for the job it performs'. That for me is the criterion. Can I live with this thing?

He went on to demonstrate how creativity is not always recognized straight away:

> There are some ugly things that I've lived with, which have grown on me. For instance a sugar bowl with a lid on, which I would have said was horrible art nouveau at one time. But it has a groove on one side so that you can easily lift it from the shelf. And the lid is a squeezed shape which nicely matches your hand when you take it off – and that's still growing in my esteem. It looked as ugly as hell to begin with, but it functions excellently.

Because they can be judged in terms of the extent to which they meet their intended function, scientific and technological products have been regarded as easier to assess than artistic work (see for instance, Gilhooly, 1982). This begs the question, What is art?

To resume the Welsh teacher's argument, 'But paintings – the ones one finds easy to live with – are those which stand the test of time, so they have to be very profound or very busy so you find more and more in them'. The idea that the longer you look at a work of art the more is revealed to you is embodied in Jackson and Messick's criterion 'condensation' outlined above.

A design lecturer described what she looked for as evidence of creativity. Initially, she said it was something about the students themselves. When recruiting new students to her courses, she was more interested in what potential students had to say than the work they brought along:

It might be the way they talk. It might not necessarily be anything manifestly creative, but if they can talk well – things they've seen or that excite them – then you know you've got something to work with. It goes back to the fact that education should encourage people not to be afraid to say how they feel. We've had students [who've enrolled] with no qualifications and hardly any designs, but by talking you know there's something there – a spark. It's about being individual. You can tell if someone puts on a pose.

She did not regard a lack of skills as especially problematic, since she could teach them.

WHO CAN ASSESS?

Approximately half the teachers believe that the only person who can legitimately assess creative work is the person who has produced it. A head of Art and Design made the point, 'On the whole I like to think it's individuals. If they are satisfied with their work, that's the main thing. If they can get others to share their view, that's fine'.

This teacher said he thought it really did have to be the individual who decided, because sometimes things are not recognized as creative at the time they are produced, but only later on, 'yet it's the same artefact. So once you get away from individuals' own estimation of their worth, who else is there that you can absolutely depend on?'.

Another member of staff pointed out that a work of art remains a work of art, even if, for example, it never leaves the empty room in which it was produced. 'If it is well executed, it will not become a lesser work, because no one has ever seen it'.

Staniszewski holds the opposing view that:

> When an artist creates a work of Art it has no intrinsic use or value; but when this artwork circulates within the systems of Art (galleries, art histories, art publications, museums, and so on) it acquires a depth of meaning, a breadth of importance, and an increase in value that is greater proportionately than perhaps anything else in the modern world.
>
> (Staniszewski, 1995, p. 28)

She argues that '"Art" is an invention of the modern era – that is, the past two hundred years. The magnificent objects and fragments and buildings created by pre-modern peoples were appropriated by our culture and transformed into Art' (Staniszewski, 1995, p. 28). The main character in Jerome K. Jerome's hilarious *Three Men in a Boat*, published in 1889, expresses the same idea:

> Why, all our art treasures of today are only the dug-up commonplaces of three or four hundred years ago . . . The 'old blue' that we hang about our walls as ornaments were the common every-day household utensils of a few centuries ago; and the pink shepherds and yellow shepherdesses that we hand round now for all our friends to gush over, and pretend they

understand, were the unvalued mantel-ornaments that the mother of the eighteenth century would have given the baby to suck when he cried . . .

. . . So it is with that china dog. In 2288 people will gush over it. The making of such dogs will have become a lost art. Our descendants will wonder how we did it, and say how clever we were. We shall be referred to lovingly as 'those grand old artists that flourished in the nineteenth century, and produced those china dogs'.

(Jerome K. Jerome, 1993 edn, pp. 53–4)

Hardly any of the teachers (6 per cent) believe that society has the legitimate right to define products as creative but, as depicted in the above extracts, it will happen anyway.

Amabile (1982) prefers a consensual assessment of creativity by experts in the field. This is ideal if the experts appreciate the value of the work. However, as she notes, difficulties may arise when new work is so original that acknowledged experts fail to recognize its merits. There are many accounts of highly creative work being initially rejected in this way. William Harvey discovered the circulation of the blood, but his theory was not accepted by all his peers and some resorted to abuse. Fabun (1968) quotes other examples. For instance, when Edison was developing electric lighting, a body of distinguished experts thought his efforts did not merit attention.

In schools and colleges, assessment is normally carried out by the teacher or lecturer, with or without written guidelines or prescribed targets, depending on the country concerned. However, there is sometimes scope for self-evaluation or peer assessment. Peer assessment tends to be common practice in design. A textiles teacher described how the whole of her class works together at the start of a project to determine suitable assessment criteria. These are then used to evaluate everyone's work when it is finished. In order not to inhibit innovative ideas, peer assessment needs to be conducted sensitively in a supportive environment, whilst not being precious about this.

The Osborn Parnes and Shallcross creative problem solving strategies are outlined in Chapter 9. These strategies are frequently used in training programmes. Shallcross's in particular is designed for classroom use. An important feature which the strategies share is that they require participants to identify and weight appropriately relevant criteria for evaluating the ideas which have been generated. This exercise offers a valuable learning experience, in which transferable skills can be acquired. Increasingly, young people will be called upon to make some quite tough decisions in real-life situations, where there is no supportive teacher on hand with a predetermined set of assessment criteria. Isn't it better that young people become skilled in self-directed assessment while still at school or college?

Another of Shallcross's approaches to assessment involves a joint discussion between teacher and student. Through careful discussion, the student becomes skilled in realistically evaluating his or her work. Importantly, this is achieved without that student's feeling of self-worth getting confused with the evaluation of the work in question (cf. the approach of Rogers, 1983). Torrance (1965) also argues for guided self-evaluation in which children realize that the teacher values their having ideas, even if they are incorrect. If a child's idea is rejected, he or she is encouraged to work out what is wrong and think of a better alternative. The ability to weigh up alternative courses of action is a valuable life-skill.

SUMMARY

To assess pupils' creativity, teachers can monitor their work, their behaviour, what they have to say – or they can administer tests. In keeping with good psychological practice the teachers involved in Project 1000 prefer to use a variety of means of assessment, although only a quarter of them regard testing as useful.

Many staff object to externally imposed testing, partly because they feel that it duplicates the continual monitoring which good teachers do automatically and partly because they do not want education to be reduced to 'teaching to a test'.

The nature of creativity is such that there can never be any definitive assessment criteria, but this does not mean that there are no relevant ones. Work which satisfies most or all relevant criteria would be of an exceedingly high standard. Much less stringent assessment procedures are appropriate for pupils' work. An important issue concerns the proportion of pupils' work which needs to be formally assessed. The criteria most popular with the teachers are imagination and originality. However, male and female staff differ significantly with regard to the criteria they value and this is in keeping with how they define creativity.

Because highly creative work necessarily extends accepted norms, it is not easy to agree who can legitimately assess it. Even experts sometimes fail to recognize the value of highly original work. In schools and colleges, guided self-evaluation is a useful assessment technique. It has the advantage of enabling children to become responsible for their own creative performance. It also enables them to develop transferable skills – skills which can be used when weighing up alternative courses of action and making decisions in other aspects of their lives.

To avoid damaging children's self-esteem, any external evaluation of children's performance needs to be carried out in a way which distinguishes between the work produced and individual feelings of self-worth. The criteria reviewed in this chapter may also be used by staff to assess their own teaching strategies.

3

Creative people

Creative persons need 'the freedom for study and preparation, the freedom for exploration and enquiry, the freedom of expression and the freedom to be themselves'.

(Stein, 1984, p. 18)

This chapter explores what teachers mean when they describe their pupils as creative and how this relates to published accounts of creative people. By virtue of their position, teachers are able to significantly affect their pupils' lives. The extent to which teachers are skilful in recognizing and supporting creative behaviour can have profound consequences for children. It is therefore very important to examine what is actually meant when teachers describe children as creative. Williams (1964) and Eberle (1966) found that elementary school teachers in the United States did not really understand what creativity involved and found it difficult to recognize it in their pupils.

One of the aims of Project 1000 was to find out what it is about their pupils that teachers identify as creative. As was demonstrated in Chapter 1, it cannot be assumed that creativity means the same thing to everyone. Indeed, it doesn't.

The teachers involved in this research really wanted to know what other staff had to say about creativity. They were equally keen to find out more about what is already known.

Activity 4

Think of an adult or a child you would describe as creative. Write a couple of paragraphs describing them. Then read on.

CALLING PEOPLE CREATIVE

A disadvantage of using a phrase like 'creative people' is that it appears to imply that some people can be creative whilst others cannot. In this chapter, the term 'creative people' is used simply as a shorthand way of referring to the individual characteristics which various investigators have found to be associated with creative production. As Cropley (1992, pp. 29–30) comments 'creativity is a complex of many factors. It involves attitudes, values, goals, and motivation, as well as special thinking skills, appropriate knowledge, and finally, talent and opportunity'. Cropley observes that whilst these can be influenced by teachers, it may be too ambitious to aim at developing high levels of creativity in all students. But it is possible to make a real difference to their levels of creativity. The extent to which 'special thinking skills' are involved will be discussed in Chapter 4 (see also Torrance and Myers, 1970; Parnes, 1992a).

One obstacle to investigating creative behaviour is that the adjective 'creative' may be attributed to an individual regardless of his or her potential or achievements.

A London primary teacher described creative people this way:

I think that everyone can get to their own particular level of creativity . . . but some people can certainly do much better. Some people have talent. Some children just respond to using a pencil. It seems so natural. It's the interest, the feedback from the task. They seem to develop so much more and put more of themselves into it.

Davis (1983, p. 18) draws attention to Maslow's (1954) distinction between 'special talent creative people' who have a special aptitude and who may or may not be well adjusted; and 'self-actualized creative people' who are mentally well adjusted, lead rich, productive lives and tend to operate in a more flexible and creative way. Davis points out that we can all aspire to the latter.

CREATIVE CHARACTERISTICS

The list of cognitive and personality characteristics which are implicated in creativity is becoming quite lengthy. Stein (1984, pp. 5–6) provides a useful résumé gleaned from the research literature. His selection is included in Table 3.1 (Stein first published the complete list in 1968).

Torrance asked a body of experts on creativity to list the characteristics they saw as typical of creative people. The ones they rated most highly are given in Table 6.1 in Chapter 6. The extent to which the Project 1000 teachers perceive themselves as having such characteristics is reported in Chapter 7 and the extent to which they want to encourage them in their students is described in Chapter 6.

Other investigators have noticed how creative people tend to work to their own time schedules. This means that highly creative pupils could be disadvantaged by externally imposed assessment deadlines. It may be that what they find hard to cope with are not the deadlines *per se*, but the fact that these are imposed by others. Amabile (1983) reports how external evaluation can be counter-productive to students' creativity. She has found that, although the situation is complex, creative performance will normally be improved when children have reasonable freedom of choice within the learning task –

Table 3.1 A sample of characteristics of creative people from an analysis of various research studies by Stein and presented in 1968

1 Is an achieving person
2 Is motivated by a need for order
3 Has a need for curiosity
4 Is self-assertive, dominant, aggressive, self-sufficient
5 Rejects repressions, is less inhibited, less formal, less conventional
6 Is persistent, likes work, is self-disciplined
7 Is independent and autonomous
8 Is constructively critical
9 Is widely informed
10 Is open to feelings and emotions
11 Is aesthetic in personal judgement
12 Can adapt values congruent with his/her environment
13 Can express feminine interests (if a male) or masculine interests (if a female) without guilt
14 Need not engage in social interactions
15 Is involved in self-fulfilment and self-realization

Source: Extracted from Stein, 1984, p. 5–6 and reproduced with kind permission.

such as which problem to attack, what materials to use and how to go about the task.

Razik (1967) describes how, in post-war America, when creativity was in great demand, initial interest in developing children's creativity was stimulated by the realization that their behaviour, their curiosity for instance, was very much like the behaviour of geniuses. This led to the view that young children were naturally creative, a view which is still pervasive, as illustrated by this primary teacher's comment:

> I think all children are creative by nature, but it is the responsibility of parents, teachers and society to encourage them so that they can make the best use of their talents or gifts. It is our duty to help them be confident and independent and these qualities will help children be creative.
>
> (primary teacher, female)

Fabun (1968) suggests that we should focus on the attributes creative people have managed to retain from childhood which others have lost, rather than trying to identify what it is about creative people that makes them different from others. What many teachers have to say reflects this, for example 'Creativity is something all children have, but which they lose as they become adults and have to study academic subjects. Intelligence is, I think inborn, but knowledge can be gained throughout life. Creativity is inborn to some extent, but most adults lose this as they mature' (FE business studies tutor, female). An infant teacher said that all she had to do was to provide the resources for creativity to happen.

However not all staff agree that young children are naturally creative:

> I am not sure young children are naturally creative. I think it has to be developed. Some children might be more creative but they may be very

untidy – you ask them what the blob on the paper is and they can tell you a wonderful story about it. I think young children are undisciplined. Being a parent helps because you can see it from that perspective too.

(primary teacher, female)

Ruth Mock, schools art adviser, argues that the notion that children can be spontaneously creative is:

far removed from the reality of the child who, satiated with an over-abundance of toys and trivial occupations, complains 'I don't know what to do'; who falls asleep at school because he [or she] has been up too late watching television or roaming the streets, who may be more likely to destroy than construct, whose visual experience is limited to comics and advertisements.

(Mock, 1970, p. 88)

An English and drama teacher who sees creativity as 'the ability to show original thought' expressed concern that schoolchildren are not always capable of original thought, 'They plagiarize TV, films, videos and computers'. Her disquiet echoes Mock's concerns. And a primary teacher commented that 'out of school, children who watch TV and video and play computer games more than they read will show less creativity, less original thought, less imagination than children who read – and this is transferred to the school situation'.

Mock (1970, p. 90) maintains that, without guidance, such children will try to reproduce the 'grotesque images' they have been induced to admire, which will not be 'free and personal' but the product of 'shoddy influences'. In similar vein, De Bono (1993, p. 17) points to the absurdity of assuming 'that everyone is naturally creative but inhibited'. Nevertheless young children, unless thwarted, do appear to exhibit considerably more imagination, curiosity and enthusiasm than many adults and these are all characteristics associated with creative productivity. Adults, on the other hand, exhibit different aspects of creativity – ones which children have to learn. This is how a head of fifth year puts it:

Creativity doesn't seem to be the same in children and adults because it's impossible to separate adults from the conditioning and experience society provides. Adults can be creative. Indeed many are, but that creativity tends to be a branching out from skills such as music which they have mastered and which has limited their freedom. Children will express ideas which are absolutely fresh to them and often in a language full of grammatical and other limitations.

A number of teachers did notice that children lost something as they grew up. The head of a Merseyside primary school said 'We've started craft, design, technology with the third year juniors – where have their ideas gone? We've tried it with the infants – all their ideas are there. They're coming up with far more creative solutions to problems. We must be doing something between top infants and third year juniors'.

A decline in creative ability associated with transitions such as the move from infants to juniors or from primary to secondary school has been quite well documented (see for instance Cropley, 1992). A major challenge for teachers is how to maintain the expressiveness, curiosity and enthusiasm of young children, whilst teaching them the other skills necessary for creativity.

Teachers gave different reasons as to why they believed children's creativity declines, for example:

> Creativity doesn't decline with age, but it might atrophy if not encouraged, if they don't find outlets for it. In terms of the national curriculum, it's very worrying because the pressure is on us to produce tangible results and teach to targets. The creative side, the expressive side, the expressive arts, are going to be pushed to one side and undervalued.

A Cambridgeshire head was convinced that

> Every child has a spark of creativity within them. It could be for language, drama, dance, movement – everybody's got something. There are children who are absolutely dull in the classroom. Out on the football field they're alive, sparkling! They've got the vocabulary. They're joyful and they can kick a ball around.

What this teacher appears to be describing is motivation engendered by the activities children enjoy. Such intrinsic motivation has been identified as a key factor in creative performance (see for instance Torrance, 1962; Amabile, 1983). In case you are wondering how this female headteacher is so aware of her pupils' performance on the football pitch, it is because she has to do the refereeing herself in the absence of a football coach. In fact my first encounter with her was on the football pitch. Our interview took place after the match!

Many accounts of highly creative people refer to their high level of motivation. Indeed, in Roe's much-quoted study of eminent scientists, the only characteristic she found they had in common was 'their driving absorption in their work' (Roe, 1952, quoted in Vernon, 1970, p. 51). As early as 1926, Cox described how 'youths who achieve eminence are characterized not only by high intellectual traits, but also by persistence of nature and effort, confidence in their abilities, and great strength or force of character' (cited in Stein, 1994c, p. 116).

Cropley (1967) cites evidence from a number of sources suggesting that very creative children come from family backgrounds which encourage the emergence of creative behaviour (for example Weisberg and Springer, 1961; Getzels and Jackson, 1962; MacKinnon, 1962). Cropley (1967; 1992) also cites case histories which support the view that parents who foster self-sufficiency, who are not over-protective and who encourage children to value their own opinions, are more successful in promoting their children's creativity than parents whose relationship with their children is cold, domineering and intrusive. The latter tend to limit the range of experiences their children have and inhibit their creative behaviour.

Paradoxically, highly creative people have emerged both from environments which may be regarded as highly favourable and highly unfavourable. A London primary teacher said she thought that creativity could arise from being driven underground – from adverse conditions. She says:

> It's probably a red herring because I don't think you can produce the conditions deliberately. I'm thinking of great artists and thinkers . . . to understand what caused it you'd have to analyse their backgrounds, as well as the things they were reacting against . . . . But I think everything being good and positive just isn't what life is. Life is also negative and bad and it's often the bad experiences which cause very strong feelings. It is probably these feelings which produce something from the individual.
>
> The very worse conditions don't produce a creative society, but they sometimes produce some very creative individuals, who have either had some very good things in their background or else they have an enormous talent which serves as an outlet for all their frustrations.

One interpretation of this paradox is that the environment has no bearing on creative outcomes. On the other hand it may be that extremely good and extremely bad conditions have something in common. According to Storr (1988) what they share is that they both offer the opportunity for solitude. Storr suggests that solitude affords the opportunity to think, to imagine: 'the capacity to be alone is a valuable resource. It enables men and women to get in touch with their deepest feelings; to come to terms with loss; to sort out their ideas; to change attitudes' (Storr, 1988, p. 62).

This tallies with Cropley's comment about non-intrusive parenting styles. Storr questions the emphasis attachment theory puts on human relationships and the way it plays down the positive effects of solitude – a significant factor in creative achievement and one which can provide an equivalent source of personal fulfilment and happiness. Interestingly, MacKinnon (1962) has noticed a significant preference for solitude amongst the highly creative architects he studied. In school there is normally little time or space for solitude. Indeed, Stein (1984, p. 27) points out that 'being different, being a loner, is frequently frowned upon'. Shallcross (1985) suggests that, to support creativity, each child should have a personal space in which to work away from the group when appropriate and a place to keep work which is being developed until such time as the child feels comfortable to share his or her new ideas with others. This suggests that it cannot be assumed (as has often been the case) that group activities are most conducive to creative work. What does appear to be important is that children are given the space to think – something which Osborn (1993) mentioned when advocating solo over group brainstorming.

Few schools have provision for children to spend time quietly working alone. Perhaps the worst provision of all is where two classes are taught formally 'back to back' in an open space originally designed for informal teaching. The kind of teaching space which would facilitate Shallcross's way of working is likely to be a spacious and flexibly furnished room or the sort of set up often provided for infants classes where classrooms cluster around a central area which can be used in a flexible way.

Another reason why difficult situations may support creativity is that they can serve as a spur to action – like 'the cutting edge that insecurity, competition and resentment supply' (Hudson, 1966, p. 232). However, it is important to note that Hudson says he is merely voicing a 'suspicion', although his ideas do have something in common with Storr's comments on the motivational power of discontent with what is and its incongruity with what might be (Storr, 1988). Bruner (1966) reminds us that the level of incongruity between present conditions and desired ones has to be pitched just right to be motivating. The primary teacher cited below suspects that difficult circumstances *per se* will not automatically result in creativity:

A person's creativity probably doesn't grow less with age, though it could possibly wither through lack of encouragement or opportunity. Perhaps the pressures of life in the inner city are such that other concerns are always foremost and creative instincts are dulled and unused. It must be very hard to lift yourself above a quagmire of financial and domestic problems and begin to fulfil your own creative aspirations.

(primary teacher, female)

An infant teacher, working in a mostly affluent catchment area, made the important point that stimulating home environments are not necessarily wealthy ones. In her opinion, interesting parents are to be found in all socio-economic groups. Such parents spend time with their children and provide opportunities for them to develop their vocabularies. Oddly enough she did not mention anything other than 'vocabularies'.

Cropley (1967) has found that highly creative children tend to be wide categorizers when coding incoming information. He describes the cognitive styles of wide and narrow categorizers. Narrow categorizers tend to code information in stereotypical ways as if it consists of large numbers of unrelated bits. On the other hand, wide categorizers tend to make novel or unusual codings which lend themselves to the kinds of cognitive leap required for productive thinking. Cropley has also noticed that highly creative people are more willing than their less creative counterparts to take intellectual risks such as guessing or hypothesizing, a tendency which Torrance (1965) has also noticed. Both McClelland (1963) and Roe (1963) also regard the willingness to take risks as a key attribute of highly creative people.

CREATIVITY AND INTELLIGENCE

A few teachers were annoyed because they had not been provided with a ready definition of creativity in their survey questionnaires. But if they had been, the differences in the way the various groups of teachers perceive creativity would not have become apparent (see Chapter 1). Since they were not provided with a ready definition of intelligence either, it was interesting to find out what it meant to them and how they saw the relationship between intelligence and creativity.

Activity 5

How do you define intelligence? Make a few notes and then read on.

Here are a few definitions of intelligence from Project 1000:

> The ability to perceive what someone is wanting from you, plus something from within you that grasps what is going on . . . outside.
>
> (primary head, female)

> The ability to formulate ideas . . . and express oneself in a way that gets the point across.
>
> (primary teacher, male)

> Association of ideas in the infant . . . . For the secondary age, the ability to show rational, logical reasoning, think for themselves, make decisions.
>
> (English and drama teacher, female)

> We are made of minerals . . . . I believe we are stones who have learned to think.
>
> (electronics lecturer, male)

> I think it's vastly different from creativity . . . . It's the capacity to understand, to unravel knowledge in useful ways. It can be broad spectrum or narrow.
>
> (head of chemistry, male)

Further examples, with teachers' definitions of creativity alongside, may be found in Fryer (1989).

Virtually all the Project 1000 teachers see intelligence and creativity as distinct, for example:

> Intelligence and creativity are not at all the same. I think that children can very often have areas of ability that don't match the rest of their skills. So, on an IQ test they would score quite low but the child may excel unexpectedly in one area. So intelligence may be a factor, but I think you can have one without the other.
>
> (primary teacher, female)

This was not too surprising, despite the fact that researchers see intelligence as an integral component of creativity. Commonly an IQ of 120 is regarded as the cut off point beyond which increasing levels of intelligence cease to have any effect on creativity. Above this level, other factors such as personality assume greater importance (see for instance Razik, 1967).

But the female head of a primary school remarked:

> I think there are a lot of similarities between creativity and intelligence. I would give the same examples for each. The trouble with intelligence is that the way it's measured is completely divorced from the children somehow. IQ and what happens in education – they don't relate really, although the tests do reflect something.

In some respects, she is echoing Stein's sentiments that

> the concept of intelligence has become reified; intelligence is no longer simply a concept but something almost tangible and capable of being 'contained' in an IQ score. All kinds of myths regarding IQ and intelligence prevail; IQs have developed lives of their own. Responsibility has been ceded to test developers.
>
> (Stein, 1994c, p. xxv)

Stein goes on to express concern that

> Practitioners . . . forget that the IQ is a measure of a child's rate of development . . . . A child's IQ is not all that one should know about a child. Among other things, one needs to know whether a child will make effective use of his or her IQ and for this, one also needs to know, from observation or test, something about the child's personality and motivation.

It was somewhat unexpected to find in Project 1000 that whilst only about a quarter of the teachers think children have no ceiling to their intelligence, two-thirds of the staff believe there is no ceiling to children's creativity. Also, whereas 70 per cent of staff believe there is some scope for developing intelligence, 90 per cent of the teachers think there is some scope for developing creativity. Some of the interviews also revealed marked differences in how creativity and intelligence are perceived. For instance a primary head thought that 'Creativity, as opposed to intelligence, needs fostering and channelling carefully. The crucial difference is that you cannot develop intelligence. You can only enhance opportunities and facilitate potential. With creativity there is more scope'.

An infant teacher felt that 'You can only go as far as your intellect will allow you. God gives you that level. You can't make someone more intelligent than they are, but I think you can improve creativity. It can grow right until you die'.

Two staff elaborated on their views. They said they saw intelligence as scientifically defined, the province of mental testers, not something teachers could influence to any great extent. But they saw creativity as much more personal, more amenable to education.

The notion of a ceiling to intelligence is at odds with the views of the British Psychological Society (1986). The Society's position on this, arrived at after reviewing both pure and applied research, is that intelligence is not immutable, but something that can be cultivated and can exist in many forms. This view has important implications, one of which is that the development of mature thinking skills is no longer the birthright of an intellectual élite.

A Merseyside art teacher sees the most creative pupils as the most intelligent. She went on to say that 'If they're brilliant at art, they're usually verbally expressive as well, so they tend to do well in English. I wouldn't say intelligent meant they could write or spell but they would be expressive both verbally and visually'.

Cropley (1967) has identified four ways in which children differ with regard to measured creativity and intelligence. Some score high on both; some low on both; some score high on intelligence, but low on creativity; others score high on creativity, but low on intelligence. It is this latter group especially which gives cause for concern. Children in this group exhibit the most behavioural difficulties and have the least comfortable passage through school. This is hardly surprising since many school systems neglect creativity. What these children excel at may well be ignored, undervalued and misunderstood, if not actively discouraged (see Chapter 6). In Project 1000, there were teachers whose perceptions of pupils match each of Cropley's categories, but hardly any of the teachers entertain all four possibilities.

Intelligence, creativity and students' work

A few teachers talked about how they thought levels of intelligence affect students' work. They each said that although more intelligent and less intelligent students could produce creative work, it tended to be the more intelligent ones who knew what it was that made the work creative. A photography teacher said that in his experience 'less bright' students would accidentally discard something which was good because they did not realize what was good about it, whereas 'a brighter kid will pick this up intuitively'. He believed that bright children were more likely to be receptive to teachers' ideas and reflect on them. In his experience they were also more willing to take risks and take advantage of 'happy accidents' which other pupils would discard.

On the other hand, 'bright' pupils would sometimes produce something that was technically correct and polished but flat, whereas a 'less bright' pupil could create something which, although rough, was very expressive. What this teacher found difficult was making the bright pupil understand the merit of the rough work and the imperfection of his or her own technically correct piece.

A male high school English teacher made some important observations about academically successful pupils and their less successful classmates, which have important implications for educational practice. For example, in his experience children skilled in written communication tend to be unwilling to 'risk anything by being creative'. On the other hand, children who are not correct in their writing but 'very imaginative, very thoughtful and extremely perceptive in their own limited way' tend to be really curious about the world, even if they don't understand it very well. Paradoxically, he described the academically successful pupils he teaches as 'creatively lazy' and boring to teach, 'they can argue about things logically and rationally; they can use a wide vocabulary and reproduce the sort of intellectual literary analysis they have picked up from the cribs, but they lack intellectual curiosity'.

He said it was difficult to have an open discussion with them. Because they thought they knew the world, they had less intellectual curiosity than their less successful peers. In written work they would choose the safe option. These children occupied the top sets and had a vested interest in maintaining their position.

A primary teacher had also noticed that some children play safe by producing unimaginative work. She said that such pupils tend to belong to 'middle class families' in which the parents are anxious for their children to do well. This parental anxiety is unwittingly transferred to the children, inhibiting their creativity. She is really concerned that a heavy reliance on formal testing as a means of assessment can exacerbate the problem.

A further example is provided by a head of music, 'Often the academically successful child is totally inhibited when asked to create music even within a fairly rigid set of guidelines. It is often the more exuberant, less bright pupil who does really well at this type of work'.

The English teacher cited above blames the examination system for the tendency of bright children to produce sterile work. In his experience a lot of high school pupils are only interested in obtaining suitable qualifications. Both Torrance (1965) and Cropley (1967) have noticed that some children play safe in this way. To counteract this tendency, Torrance recommends setting at least some tasks which are not assessed.

In higher education it is quite common to find young people, who have been very successful in school examinations, being afraid of putting their ideas forward, for fear of being wrong. Stein (1993) has found that students make remarkable progress when this kind of fear is removed. Clearly if we want to encourage children's creativity, we need to give academically successful children the opportunity of making mistakes and taking intellectual risks, at least some of the time.

It is just as important to enable pupils who have good ideas, but lack the skills to communicate them formally, to acquire such skills. In the absence of good written communication skills, these students become frustrated and in extreme cases resort to abuse and even violence.

In what ways are children intelligent or creative?

When asked how he defined intelligence, a Project 1000 social care lecturer said he would not want to: 'My background is with people with learning difficulties. You realize from this that a person can be very good at something, but atrocious at something else'. To illustrate his point he contrasted those of his students who could not read, but who could quickly learn to cope with finding their way around a strange city, with those who were competent readers but had little sense of direction. His comments are echoed by Gardner (1993) who argues that the wrong questions are being asked about intelligence. He maintains that we should not be asking about children's levels of intelligence, but in what ways they are intelligent. Treffinger has made a similar point with regard to creativity. In the next chapter we shall be exploring creativity as a process, rather than an attribute.

SUMMARY

In this book the term creative people is not meant to imply that some people can be creative and others cannot. It is simply a convenient way of referring to individual characteristics associated with creativity. People may also be described as creative when this is not justified, but this happens with other forms of labelling too.

Curiosity, imagination and enthusiasm are qualities frequently associated with both creativity and very young children. Whilst these are important, they are not the only attributes necessary for creativity. A key question for teachers is how to help young people retain these childhood qualities, whilst developing the other skills and knowledge they need in order to be creative.

Although various characteristics have been cited as indicative of creative people, perhaps the most pervasive feature of highly creative people is their persistence – their willingness to work hard in pursuit of their goals.

It was rather surprising to find how creativity, intelligence and IQ are perceived by some staff. Clearly this is something which needs addressing in teacher training.

Creativity can emerge from both highly favourable and highly unfavourable environments. There is some evidence that making provision for each child to become immersed in a project he or she finds fascinating can be helpful. Whether the child works on this alone or with others depends on the child, the task and the situation. This does not mean that lessons need to be lacking in pace, guidance, ground rules or structure. Normally the reverse is the case. But learning experiences which allow children little scope to think for themselves are likely to be counter-productive.

To develop their creativity, children need to be able to test out their ideas and sometimes find them wanting, without this affecting their self-esteem or their future educational prospects. At present many educational systems favour those who produce technically correct, but not necessarily imaginative, work. We shall increasingly need people who can do both.

4

Being creative

To make a prairie it takes a clover and one bee,
One clover, and a bee,
And revery,
The revery alone will do,
If bees are few.
                    (Emily Dickinson, *Poems*, c.1862–86)

The purpose of this chapter is to explore what is involved in being creative. It draws attention to work which offers the most promising insights, suggests new conventions in the use of terminology and proposes the discarding of prejudices and archaic beliefs in favour of more plausible explanations. Promising findings are brought together and integrated to provide a fresh account of the creative process.

In this book 'creative thinking' is used as a convenient shorthand for the kind of thinking which results in the production of creative ideas and artefacts (as defined by the kinds of criteria discussed in Chapter 2). It is not meant to imply that any peculiar or unusual processes are involved, since there is no evidence to suggest this.

Unnecessary muddle has been caused by the careless use of the term 'creative' in the literature (see also Stein, 1994c and Chapter 1). It is common practice to use this term to refer to both creative thinking as a whole, and more specifically to what is frequently called divergent thinking. Confusion would be avoided if its use were restricted to the former.

The chapter begins by exploring creative thinking using a wide angle lens, taking in the big picture, before focusing on the finer detail. In doing this, I will outline the competing explanations and offer my personal view as a psychologist.

THE BIG PICTURE

We may think of creative thinking as an attention-directing activity. Ordinary cognitive processes (that is, perception, memory, learning, language and reasoning) are employed in various ways in pursuit of original, appropriate, useful, valuable (etc.) ideas and products; or in the re-vamping of old ones in new ways.

There is much debate about the extent to which creative thinking involves the adoption of specific strategies and what such strategies might involve. Building on the landmark work of Guilford (for instance Guilford, 1977), many investigators have concluded that creative thinking involves both thinking broadly or generatively, as when generating lots of possible ideas, and then narrowly (analytically or critically), as when homing in on a particular idea or solution.

Most commonly the term *divergent* is used to refer to the generative aspect and *convergent* to the analytical aspect. Indeed, various creativity development programmes such as the Osborn-Parnes Creative Problem Solving Programme (see Chapter 9) are based on an iterative process of convergent and divergent *thinking*.

Whilst not invalidating the efficacy of such programmes, there are now good psychological reasons why it would be more appropriate to abandon the popular terms *divergent* and *convergent* in favour of the more accurate descriptors *generative* and *critical* respectively (see below). It also seems likely that a more accurate explanation of the generative and critical aspects of creative thinking is that they represent *different foci of attention* (broad and narrow) rather than different modes of thinking.

According to Hocevar (1981), creativity is most frequently described in the literature in terms of divergent thinking. Only about half the Project 1000 teachers see creativity in this way.

The association of the terms divergent and convergent with creativity have been attributed to Guilford (for instance, Weisberg, 1993). Convergence, in particular, has traditionally been associated with *logical reasoning* (see for instance Paul, 1993).

There is a fairly widespread assumption that logical reasoning is the natural or *correct* way of reasoning. However, Johnson-Laird (1983; 1988) provides convincing evidence that in everyday life, when we think logically, we do not generally follow the strict rules of logic, although we can do so if we wish. More usually we step outside the strict confines of the problem as stated to draw on our existing knowledge of the world.

One way in which Johnson-Laird (1988, p. 219) illustrates his point is with the following example. He describes how we make sense of the sentences 'The victim was stabbed to death in a cinema. The suspect was on an express train to Edinburgh when the murder occurred' by going beyond the information contained in the two sentences to draw on what we already know about cinemas, express trains and people's inability to be in two places at once. Such a strategy steps outside of the bounds of logical reasoning.

It may seem pedantic to call for a rejection of outmoded terminology, such as convergent and divergent, and for consistency in the use of words like creative, but it is important that explanations of the creative process reflect as nearly as possible our best understanding of it. Explanations in terms of *attention* make sense, given what is known about human cognition.

THE FINER DETAIL – IMAGINATION AND CREATIVE THINKING

Human cognition is an active, making sense activity. Even when we *see* physical objects we are interpreting incoming information in terms of what we already know. We are only aware that we are interpreting, when we realize our conclusions are wrong (for instance Roth, 1978). A simple way of demonstrating this is to ask a number of pupils to each describe a particular scene or scenario. They will probably all give different accounts.

Building on Craik's work on mental models, Johnson-Laird puts forward a powerful argument that when we reason we do so by building and comparing both real and imaginary models of the world. He maintains that in straightforward situations, what we are doing is making sense of a situation by constructing a single mental model – an explanation or image that we find acceptable. In more puzzling situations, we construct a number of alternative mental models and search among them for a solution. Johnson-Laird sees such models as flexible and dynamic.

He describes how, in quite straightforward situations, we are scarcely aware that we are solving problems since this happens so rapidly, but in more complicated ones we become much more aware of our thinking processes (Johnson-Laird, 1988). Indeed we are solving problems much more frequently than we realize. Not all psychologists accept a mental models explanation of human cognition, but a lot of alternative accounts are less robust in the face of criticism.

Johnson-Laird recognizes that his mental models explanation of human cognition calls into question Piaget and Inhelder's popular account of human reasoning (see also Bryant and Trabasso, 1971; Donaldson, 1978; 1982). Goswami's findings also call Piaget's account into question. She has found that children as young as three can reason by analogy, although they can do this much more effectively in familiar knowledge domains (Goswami, 1992).

IMAGINATION AND CREATIVITY

In general, cognitive psychology has tended to shy away from words like 'imagination' in favour of less emotive ones like 'images' and 'mental models'. And of course imagination (at least as it is traditionally understood) encompasses more than images or mental models might suggest (see for instance White, 1990). Johnson-Laird does at least refer to imagination a few times. Indeed it is his account of reasoning as an imaginative process (Johnson-Laird, 1987) which adds considerable weight to the view that imagination deserves a higher profile in education than even most creativity literature would suggest (Fryer, 1989; 1994a). Johnson-Laird, it must be said, describes creative thinking at a more strategic level of analysis (see below).

Traditionally, imagination and creativity have been seen as closely connected. For example, Wheeler-Brownlee (1985) describes creativity as the public expression of imagination, the latter being essentially a private phenomenon. Most accounts of creative thinking stress the significance of imagination (for instance Osborn, 1993) but it is its relevance to generative rather than critical elements which is normally acknowledged.

However, Paul (1993, p. 28) provides an excellent account of the close links between logic and creating (something which tends to be largely forgotten):

> We approach virtually everything in our experience as something that can be . . . 'decoded' by the power of our minds to create a conceptualization . . . . We do this so routinely and automatically that we do not typically recognize ourselves as engaged in processes of reasoned creation . . . . So we see [things as] 'trees', 'clouds', 'grass', 'roads', 'people', 'men', 'women' and so on. We apply these concepts intuitively, as if no rational, creative act were involved . . . we study living organisms to construct 'bio-logic', that is, to establish ways to conceptualize and make valid inferences about life forms.

Paul makes a similar point about 'social arrangements' and 'sociologic', pointing out that 'no one is born with these logical structures . . . everyone must "create" them'.

Most Project 1000 teachers do see imagination as integral to creativity (see Table 1.1).

ATTITUDES TO IMAGINATION

In Project 1000, it is the male teachers and those teaching science, maths and technology who most value imaginative young people. But their view is not shared by all the staff, 9 per cent (94) of whom do not value them. They perceive the most imaginative pupils as the most ineffectual. Such a view is in stark contrast with the demand for such individuals from successful, modern organizations.

It is not entirely surprising to find that imagination is not highly regarded by all teachers and lecturers. For centuries, the ability to imagine has been the subject of discrimination, suspicion, even hatred (see for instance, Kearney, 1988; Egan, 1992). Their excellent historical accounts of the varied fortunes of imagination go a long way towards explaining why imagination has been marginalized in education and how the arts/science split has come about.

Egan (1992) illustrates the value of imagination by describing how oral cultures have traditionally used their imagination to create vivid myths to transmit important information from one generation to the next. Vivid images have been used, he says, because they are easier to remember than less interesting material and because they have the capacity to arrest our attention, something which has been borne out by psychological research (for instance, Cohen, Eysenck and LeVoi, 1986). Egan suggests that it was no accident that the mother of the Muses – who were the goddesses of the arts – was

Mnemosyne, the goddess of memory and he points out that 'Museum came to mean a place of education and research' (Egan, 1992, p. 12).

Storr (1988) puts forward an even more powerful argument as to why imaginative skills should be valued. He maintains that our very survival as a species depends on them. Storr sees imagination as biologically adaptive, because it allows us to compare our current situation with what is possible. It also affords us a tremendous flexibility, something which other animals do not have. Such flexibility allows us to adapt to and survive in a whole range of climatic conditions, including intense heat, extreme cold – outer space, even.

Despite this (or perhaps because of it) the human capacity to imagine has been so much the subject of abuse that it has even been regarded as 'incorrigibly wicked' (Kearney, 1988, p. 43). Kearney points out that imagination has been regarded in quite similar ways in both the Hebrew and Hellenic traditions. He describes (1988, p. 39, original emphasis) how, in the Hebrew story of the Creation:

> Original Sin . . . marks imagination from its inception. The Knowledge of Good and Evil, which the serpent promises will make Adam and Eve 'like Gods', is henceforth identified with [people's] ability to imagine a world of [their] own making . . . . The initial realization of [people's] imaginative potential would thus appear to correspond . . . with both an *ethical* consciousness of good and evil and an *historical* consciousness of past and future.

Kearney (1988, p. 80) compares the account of the creation with the Hellenic myth of Prometheus, pointing out that 'pro-metheus' means 'fore-sight . . . the power to anticipate the future by projecting an horizon of imaginary possibilities'. Kearney describes how 'Prometheus stole fire from the gods and bestowed it upon [people]'. For this he was punished by Zeus, but 'With the use of this stolen fire, [people were] able to invent [their] own world'.

Kearney points out that both accounts describe imagination as a 'rebellion against the divine order of things'. Clearly anyone wishing to support imagination in teaching and learning has a long history of discrimination with which to contend! (see also Stein, 1983).

Imagination has not always been considered a godlike attribute. Its association with art, which in Plato's day tended to mimic reality, devalued imagination in his eyes. Plato distinguishes between 'the reasoning faculty that can know the truth and the faculty of imagination that can only *mimic* the appearance of things' (Egan, 1992, p. 14, original emphasis).

Egan describes how imagination was further devalued by Descartes. It is perhaps fittingly ironic that it was in a dream that the twenty-three-year-old Descartes 'saw the possibility of a unified body of scientific knowledge . . . based on a single coherent system of principles; in contrast with the scholastic theory that the sciences were separate' (Lucas, 1963, p. 113).

Egan (1992, p. 19, original emphasis) tells how Descartes' student, Malebranche, wrote a treatise in which he describes 'the senses, the imagination and the passions as obstacles to be overcome by reason in *its* search for truth'. Egan points out that Bacon's view of imagination was similar – it 'hardly produces sciences', but only poetry or art, which is 'to be accounted rather as a pleasure or play of wit than a science'. Similarly, according to Egan, Addison saw imagination as 'not a serious part of the mind's equipment, but rather . . . a kind of ornamental delight . . . [which] offers 'a kind of refreshment' to the serious and hard-working understanding and reason'.

Egan (1992, pp. 15, 21) points out that, although Aristotle saw artistic imagination as representing 'universal features of human experience', imagination retained its low status until the late eighteenth century when Hume reluctantly acknowledged the role played by imagination in transforming 'fleeting, partial and constantly changing' perceptions of the world into 'stable, clear, constant image[s] of the world'. From then on, the status of imagination amongst philosophers improved, with Kant recognizing its meaning-making function in making sense of our perceptions in the light of our knowledge and experience. This sounds similar to Johnson-Laird's (1987) argument about reasoning, which he describes as a semantic process which relies on imagining states of affairs and seeking counter-examples.

Egan (1992, p. 25) describes how we have 'inherited from the Romantics a sense of imagination belonging to the arts and as something distinct from the functions of our reason', although this was not a view held by Wordsworth.

The historical account given by Egan usefully charts the origins of the anti-imagination prejudice and the damaging arts/science split, which are still pervasive. Even today, the arts, which are popularly associated with imagination, are frequently marginalized (Fryer, 1989; 1994a). Teachers of the arts often have to fight for inclusion in the curriculum, timetable space, suitable teaching accommodation and resources. Yet modern science needs people who are skilled in imagining. Quantum physics, for example, is becoming increasingly concerned with uncertainty, paradox and probability, not to mention superstrings! There are many famous examples of scientific breakthroughs brought about through the use of imagery, not least Einstein imagining himself travelling on a beam of light when devising his theory of relativity (for instance Amabile, 1983).

Furthermore, the arts and sciences have much more in common than is normally acknowledged. Both mathematics and poetry rely on highly symbolic codes. It would be in the interests of good education to throw off early prejudices and take steps to mend the artificial arts/science split. At the same time it is worth remembering that it is perfectly possible to teach the arts, and indeed all other subjects, in a mechanistic way which allows little opportunity for children to construct alternative mental models and make comparisons – in other words, with little opportunity *to imagine*.

Given a long history of neglect in formal education, we may not have yet discovered all the uses to which our imaginative capacity can be put. For instance we do not know a great deal about the use of 'visualization' techniques. One way they have been used, however, has been by athletes who have used them to envisage challenges and plan their strategies in advance (for instance Parnes, 1992a; 1992b). Merritt (1994) describes the benefits of using imaging techniques in organizational settings.

Storr describes how the capacity to make comparisons between our current state and what is possible may make us discontented with the present, but it is precisely this discontent which spurs us into action. Bruner (1966) also recognizes the motivational power of the incongruity between what is and what might be, as discussed below.

THE MOTIVATION TO BE CREATIVE

McVicker Hunt (1960) and Bruner (1966) describe how tasks which are just a little different from or more difficult than previous tasks motivate us to tackle them. To be motivating, the level of incongruity between previous and new tasks has to be pitched just right. If new tasks are too difficult, they are frustrating. If they are too easy, they are boring.

There are clear implications for classroom teaching and creativity. The old-fashioned, factory-style schooling criticized by Glasser (1993) is ill-suited to motivating pupils in this way. Whilst whole class teaching fulfils other important functions, it needs to be complemented with a range of assignments which children find intrinsically motivating. These will be varied in terms of content, learning mode and level of difficulty – to stretch pupils just enough to provide the requisite incongruity. Highly able children will need significant challenges to maintain their motivation.

Giving pupils a certain amount of choice amongst such options helps them have a sense of ownership of and responsibility for their work. The value of a sense of ownership for motivating pupils is acknowledged both by Glasser and, in the present study, by a high school head of chemistry (see Chapter 7).

Intrinsic motivation has been cited as a major catalyst for creativity (for instance Torrance, 1962; Amabile, 1983). Torrance (1962) describes how creative individuals cannot stop working because they cannot stop thinking. They find nothing more enjoyable than work which uses their creative abilities.

There may well be a cumulatively positive effect on children's creative output if they are given the opportunity to work on tasks they find intrinsically motivating, at least for some of the time. The evidence suggests that we learn skills by actively using them. Johnson-Laird (1983) points out that the way musicians learn how to improvise is by improvising. Creative problem solving training programmes which actively involve participants in thinking creatively do indeed produce improvements in such abilities (see for instance Parnes, 1992a). Also, Paul (1993, p. 39) observes that 'It is stimulating intellectual work that develops the intellect . . . . Fitness of mind, intellectual excellence, is the result'. Should we be surprised if people become more creative by creating?

We may think of imagination as a pervasive component of creative thinking, but on another level creativity can be envisaged as a strategy. Returning to the big picture, some examples of strategic accounts of creative thinking are considered next. ⸴

STRATEGIC ACCOUNTS OF CREATIVE THINKING

Wallas's four stage model

Various *stage* models attempt to describe how we go about thinking creatively. Perhaps the most publicized account is Wallas's four stage theory (Wallas, 1926; extracts reprinted in Vernon, 1970), yet there are good reasons for thinking that this may not be the most accurate description of what happens.

Wallas devised his theory on the basis of various highly creative people's accounts of how they came up with creative ideas. Indeed, one of them, the mathematician Poincaré, also proposed quite a similar account based on his own experience (Gilhooly, 1982). But to what extent can people describe their creative thinking retrospectively? The accuracy of self-reports on problem solving strategies has been called into question by Wason (1978).

Wallas's explanation of creative thinking involves four 'stages'. The first, when a problem is being investigated, he calls 'preparation'; the second, when the problem is not receiving any attention – 'incubation'; the third, where the ideas appear – 'illumination'; and the fourth stage – 'verification'. Wallas thought that illumination was preceded by an awareness that the problem was about to be solved and he called this 'intimation'. To illustrate the phenomena of incubation and inspiration, Wallas cites an account by Helmholtz who noticed that 'after previous investigation of the problem "in all directions . . . happy ideas come unexpectedly without effort like an inspiration"' (Wallas, 1926, in Vernon, 1970, p. 91).

Wallas's theory has been criticized for being too rigid, even though he did envisage the stages as overlapping – an individual, he said, might be incubating on one aspect of a problem, at the same time as preparing for or verifying another element. Johnson-Laird (1988) maintains that there is no evidence that people solve problems in the way Wallas has suggested.

Inspiration, incubation and alternative explanations

Notions of inspiration and incubation, employed by Wallas and others, have not served creativity well. Instead, they have created a counter-productive air of mystery. But we can hardly blame Wallas for this, since the word inspiration goes back to Greek mythology. The Muses, the nine daughters of Zeus, who ruled over the arts and sciences, were thought to breathe creative ideas into artists – hence the term 'inspiration' (Weisberg, 1993). Ochse (1990) suggests that there are too many subjective accounts of sudden inspiration or 'insights' associated with creativity, to simply dismiss them.

Like Wason, Ochse doubts whether the explanations people give about moments of insight truly reflect the cognitive processes involved. He distinguishes between subjective descriptions which may be quite accurate, and subjective explanations which are unlikely to be. Also Ochse has noticed that most accounts of inspiration describe how the individual involved was in a state of low arousal, as in dreaming, when inspiration occurred. Such states, he argues, assist the search for creative solutions, because they serve to widen the attention span. This allows us to entertain ideas outside the confines of the problem on which we have been narrowly focusing up to then. Ochse's explanation of inspiration sounds plausible and is compatible with Mednick's view that creative solutions arise from the connecting of remote, previously unassociated ideas, even though he is addressing this phenomenon from quite a different perspective (for instance Mednick, 1962).

Of course, a low state of arousal is not always necessary for previously unrelated ideas to come together. It can also happen when experts from one field apply their specialist knowledge to problems in another field. A key creative problem solving technique involves forced association between apparently unrelated stimuli (for instance Geschka, 1994).

Simply taking a break, after some concentrated effort on a problem, can also have the same effect of widening the span of attention to allow in unrelated ideas. Woodworth and Schlosberg (1954) identify this as a fruitful strategy for locating creative solutions, but the reason they give is that it allows inappropriate trains of thought to decay. Simon (1966) expresses the same idea which he describes as selective forgetting. He says this allows more relevant information to be retrieved.

But breaks may be more apparent than real since people may continue to creatively worry (Olton, 1979). This is precisely what Poincaré did, according to Weisberg. In an interesting experiment, Murray and Denny (1969) found that taking a break helped a low-ability group, but was counter-productive for a high-ability group. They suggest that this is because for the low-ability group, it provided the opportunity for unhelpful ideas to decay, but for the high-ability group it was disruptive, since it broke the continuity of their problem solving strategy.

Weisberg cites evidence to suggest that creative discovery does not involve great leaps of insight. The process is more incremental. Ochse (1990) agrees, pointing out that important creative outcomes often have no clear start or finish, and can involve much uneventful labour which may last for months or even years, during which time valid insights may occur, but mixed up with ones which are not valid or useful. In view of this, it might be appropriate to drop notions of inspiration and incubation.

Torrance's research model of creative thinking

Torrance (1965, in Sternberg, 1988, p. 47) maintains that creative thinking involves 'sensing difficulties, problems, gaps in information, missing elements, something askew; making guesses and formulating hypotheses about these deficiencies; evaluating and testing these guesses and hypotheses; possibly revising and retesting them; and finally communicating the results'. His account has much in common with the process of normal research. Here, Torrance is referring specifically to intellectual rather than artistic creativity. Weisberg (1986) maintains that the process is similar in both.

Johnson-Laird's model of the creative process

It will be evident from the early part of this chapter that Johnson-Laird has made a significant contribution to our understanding of human cognition. He is also highly critical of popular explanations of the creative thinking process.

He recognizes that there must be 'some given building blocks' since one 'cannot create out of nothing' (Johnson-Laird, 1988, p. 255). He argues that inherent in being creative is a lack of a precise goal, but there are certain constraints or criteria which have to be met (cf. Paul, 1993). He illustrates this with various examples, one of which is poetry. Essentially, Johnson-Laird maintains that, whilst there is considerable freedom in composing a poem, if all the criteria were flouted, it would be unrecognizable as a poem (see also Chapter 2).

Johnson-Laird (1988, p. 268) puts forward three possible models of the creative process, including a multistage model, which he suggests offers the most plausible explanation of creative achievement in science and the arts. He describes this as a process in which 'The creator generates ideas, making use of at least some initial constraints'. Then there may be 'revision or elaboration' involving constraints which were not initially available. He gives the example of testing a hypothesis. The initial design may have certain limitations, but as yet there is no data. Later on when there is some data, one may wish to improve the original research design. This explanation has similarities with Torrance's research model above, as well as the Osborn-Parnes and Shallcross accounts of creative problem solving (see Chapter 9).

Johnson-Laird's mental models explanation of human cognition is entirely compatible with his explanation of creative thinking, since they operate at different levels of explanation. Despite this and although he clearly recognizes the role of imagination in reasoning (Johnson-Laird, 1987), he does not appear to have explicitly stated the connections between creation, imagination and mental models.

Motamedi (1982) has produced a strategic model of creative thinking which he describes as a journey. For a useful résumé of other strategic models of creative thinking, see Guilford (1977). Many strategic models of creativity use the term *stage*. Since this has connotations of Piagetian invariant stages, the term *phase* might be a more accurate descriptor.

CREATIVE THINKING – ORDINARY THINKING

It seems highly likely that we all have the capacity to think creatively. As Guilford (1950) argues, most psychologists would probably agree that creative people do not have peculiar gifts. All individuals have the same capabilities in varying degrees, in the absence of pathologies. So it is possible for anyone to be creative to an extent.

In keeping with the spirit of Guilford's argument, Perkins (1981, p. 274) maintains that no unusual or special thinking processes are involved in being highly creative. It simply involves 'the mind's best work'. Mock (1970, p. 18) makes a similar observation about imagination which she describes as 'the creative faculty of the mind in its highest aspect'. Perkins goes on to describe creativity as 'a process of gradually selecting from an infinity of possibilities an actual product . . . . The process of selecting is roundabout because of limits on human mental resources and the human will to push these resources to their limits'. This, he says, involves 'planning', 'abstracting', 'undoing' and 'making means into ends' (Perkins, 1981, p. 276). He likens being creative to putting the top on a pyramid of possibilities, but is at pains to point out that this is not quite as daunting as it might be, since a lot of the groundwork has already been done. Clearly it is sometimes necessary to undo the groundwork.

What is worrying is that most educational systems only address a very narrow range of intellectual skills (Guilford, 1977; and others). Guilford (1977) devised a 3D 'Structure of the Intellect' model to demonstrate that we have many more intellectual abilities than either IQ tests measure or education addresses. He points out that some of these were recognized by Binet, but not included in his IQ tests, because Binet considered them irrelevant to his purpose at that time.

According to Guilford, in both IQ testing and education there has been a tendency to focus on comprehension and understanding rather than productive thinking, which is of greater importance in problem solving. De Bono makes a similar point. However, along with Torrance, Parnes, Hermann and others, Guilford recognizes that creativity requires critical skills as well as productive skills and he stresses the need for a balanced approach to education in which the development of all such skills is encouraged.

There is some evidence that people become highly skilled thinkers by becoming immersed for a significant period in an area of study which fascinates them – something which Torrance has long recommended. The evidence for this comes from psychological and educational research as well as biographical accounts of individuals who have produced outstanding work. The value of deep learning has also been demonstrated by Entwistle (1987). Children need the opportunity to get deeply immersed in their work. This is not always easy in a traditional classroom setting. Teachers' suggestions for how this might be achieved are given in later chapters.

There is dispute about whether skilled thinking in one area is transferable to other areas. The problem is confounded by the fact that to think effectively in a particular domain, you have to have the skills and knowledge specific to that domain. Apart from this, there does not appear to be any good reason why thinking skills learned through application in one domain cannot be transferred to another. The point is that the individual concerned needs to realize their relevance. The ability to recognize analogies between one area and another has been cited as a valuable skill in creativity (Gordon, 1961; Weisberg, 1993) (see also Chapter 9).

POSTSCRIPT

Different schools of thought have offered conflicting explanations of the creative process. Whilst healthy debate is good, there is some evidence in the creativity literature of groundless criticism and an apparent failure to acknowledge relevant research data – a state of affairs which could be quite damaging.

Close examination reveals that there is rather more commonality among the various perspectives than is usually recognized. This has made it possible to use material normally associated with one explanation of the creative process to support another viewpoint. However, in the interests of brevity and clarity, elaboration of this issue has been avoided, since it would result in a very different book.

SUMMARY

As in Chapter 3, the adjective 'creative' has been used simply as a shorthand device for describing the thinking and other processes associated with creative production. There is no evidence that any unusual processes are involved. It has been argued that the inconsistent use of the term 'creative' is a continuing source of confusion.

If we draw together the various contributions and ideas presented in this chapter, it is possible to envisage a simple model of creative thinking in which imagination (in the sense of mental models) is pervasive. Attention has been drawn to the historical reasons why imagination is frequently undervalued in education, something which may well account for the long-standing and counter-productive arts/sciences divide.

Because of its traditional link with logic, the use of the term *convergent thinking* to describe part of the thinking strategy used in creative production, underplays the role of imagination in thinking. Psychologists, such as Johnson-Laird, have demonstrated that when we solve problems we frequently go outside strict logic to draw on what we already know. Also, even logical explanations are based on conceptualizations. To take account of all of these, it is suggested that we replace the term *convergent* with *analytical* or *critical*, and replace *divergent* with *generative*. It is further suggested that critical and generative thinking may be regarded as attention-directing strategies, as opposed to qualitatively different kinds of thinking.

It has also been argued that it is time to drop the archaic notions of *inspiration* and *incubation*, in favour of more plausible explanations; and that *stages* in the thinking process be replaced by the less static term *phases*.

It is useful to consider how incongruent tasks can motivate students to perform them, as discussed by Bruner, and the role imagination can play in alerting us to such incongruity, as discussed by Storr.

To encourage their creativity, students should be given plenty of opportunities to imagine – in the sense of thinking for themselves. Becoming deeply immersed in areas of the curriculum in which they are most interested and getting practice in seeing analogies between one situation and another will also help. Finally, it appears that a good way for students to learn how to be creative is by creating.

5

Patterns and relationships

Most women are introspective. We look within for happiness: 'Am I in love? . . . Am I communicating my feelings? . . . Am I emotionally and creatively fulfilled?'

Most men are outrospective: 'Did my team win? . . . Do people think I make a lot of money? . . . How's my car?'

(Rita Rudner, *Rita Rudner's Guide to Men*, 1994, p. 1)

One reason why the above extract from the American comedienne Rita Rudner makes us smile, is because it reflects typical differences in male/female perspectives on the world. Traditional roles are shifting. Indeed, there have always been cultural variations in the roles men and women occupy (see for instance Mead, 1962), but at the same time differences remain in the way men and women see the world.

Collings and Smithers (1984) have noticed that females tend to be *person-oriented* and males more ideas or *object-oriented*. They have also found that on the whole science choosers tend to be object-oriented, whilst non-science choosers tend to be person-oriented, although Collings (1978) found that female sixth formers opting for biology were more person-oriented than those opting for the physical sciences. According to Collings, *person orientation* describes a preference for dealing with, or involving oneself in, emotional, social or interpersonal issues as distinct from impersonal ones. Collings and Smithers maintain that person orientation is not the same as sociability or extroversion. It simply means being most comfortable thinking about social, emotional and personal matters. It does not necessarily involve being socially skilled or seeking company.

Helgesen (1990) cites a number of studies, mostly in the field of management, which bear out Collings' and Smithers' findings. In particular, she contrasts Mintzberg's description of successful male managers with her own case studies of successful women entrepreneurs. She has noticed that the female managers' style of operating reflects their concern for human relationships, whilst the male managers in Mintzberg's investigation adopted a mainly instrumental approach – seeing people as essentially a means to an end. It is true that Mintzberg's data was collected over twenty years ago, but this is not the only example of this phenomenon. A somewhat newer example she cites is Greenhalgh's (1985) study of gender differences in negotiating styles where:

> women's values for interdependence and mutuality make them treat negotiations within the context of continuing relationships that require contact, interaction and agreement. By contrast, men's focus on independence, competitiveness and autonomy makes them more likely to see negotiations as an opportunity for winning or [beating] an opponent than for collaborating or building a relationship.
>
> (Helgesen, 1990, pp. 247–8)

PERCEPTIONS OF CREATIVITY

What was quite unexpected, since it did not appear to have been reported before, was to find that the male and female teachers involved in Project 1000 see creativity quite differently from one another – in ways which reflect the personal perspective of females, on the one hand, and the less personal perspective of males on the other.

This conclusion emerges from a range of measures (Fryer, 1989; 1993; Fryer and Collings, 1991a). For example, the female teachers are more inclined than the males to see creativity in terms of self-expression, imagination and an awareness of beauty. When assessing pupils' work for creativity, they are much more likely than the male teachers to consider the extent to which the work expresses depth of feeling, depth of thought, originality and experience. But the male tutors are more aware than the females of the role critical thinking plays in creativity. They are also more inclined to evaluate children's work *per se*, than to assess whether it reflects the children's experience. Men value elegance as a criterion more than women do.

It must be remembered that all the Project 1000 findings discussed in this chapter relate to groups. Group results always mask within-group and individual differences. For example, there is no suggestion that every female teacher in the investigation sees creativity in personal terms, simply that a significant majority of them do. With regard to different subject groups, exactly the same kind of pattern emerges. When we look at different subject teachers' perceptions, we find that every subject group envisages creativity in more personal terms than do those teaching maths, science and technology. This finding holds good when male and female subject teachers are considered separately.

PREFERRED WAYS OF TEACHING

As might be expected, the female teachers generally prefer a pupil-oriented approach to teaching, whilst the male staff prefer an instrumental approach. In the context of this investigation, being pupil-oriented includes believing that anyone can be creative and that creativity can be developed. Pupil-oriented teachers want their pupils to be aware of the world in which they live and to understand it. They want them to be competent in a range of skills, including expressive skills, be able to manipulate knowledge, and think both critically and intuitively. They want pupils to be able to find things out for themselves, to express their feelings and respond empathically to others. Such staff think that teaching should be fitted to every child, and that pupils should take a role in planning the curriculum and have some choice in how they learn. They see free expression work and integrated project work as useful means of achieving their educational objectives. The sources of data they value for assessing creativity include pupils' ideas and questions, the work they produce and their behaviour.

In this investigation, 'instrumental' involves not attaching much importance to the things pupil-oriented staff value. Instead there is a greater concern for the mastery of basic skills, achievement of high academic standards and punishment of misbehaviour. Regular practice and regular testing are regarded as the most useful means of achieving educational objectives.

Groups teaching general subjects, the arts and nursing are more in favour of pupil-oriented teaching than are the maths, science and technology staff, with the nursing tutors being the most pupil-oriented. The views of the business studies and humanities teachers tend, on the whole, to be more aligned with those of the maths, science and technology staff, but there are variations from scale to scale. The subject group findings hold good when males and females are considered separately.

TEACHERS MOST AND LEAST POSITIVE ABOUT CREATIVITY

By means of a statistical technique it was possible to ascertain the percentages of staff who were most, least and moderately oriented to creativity (see also Chapter 1). The technique involves some of the members of the entire group of teachers being anonymously assigned to each of the two extreme groups (i.e. most and least interested in creativity) on the basis of criteria derived from the existing body of knowledge on creativity and statistical analyses.

Attempts to identify the percentages in each of the two extreme groups were somewhat thwarted, because only one teacher out of the 1028 who took part in the investigation was found to be completely negative about creativity – an educationally useful finding in itself. But in terms of the analysis, it meant that the criteria for membership of the 'least positive' group had to be relaxed a little. The criteria for the 'most positive' group remained stringent. Essentially the criteria all relate to views about creativity.

This technique cannot normally assign teachers to groups with complete accuracy, but it is possible to know how accurately this has been carried out. In this instance, 87 per cent were correctly allocated (which is a respectably high proportion). Further details are given in Fryer (1989) and Fryer and Collings (1991a).

In Project 1000, staff who are really positive about creativity comprise 17 per cent (176) of the total group of 1028 and those who are least positive comprise 9 per cent (94), with the rest somewhere between the two extremes.

The next step was to find out what else distinguished between teachers most and least positive about creativity. This was found to be (with one minor exception) a set of opinions about teaching and learning (see Table 5.1 and Fryer and Collings, 1991a).

As can be seen from Table 5.1, the questionnaire items (variables) which best differentiate between the two extreme groups (most and least oriented to creativity) are a set of attitudes and beliefs – views which mostly reflect a pupil-oriented approach to education.

Table 5.1   The top ten items which differentiate teachers most positive about creativity from those least positive (N = 1028)

Wish to deepen pupils' understanding of the world
Believe all pupils can be creative
Try to match teaching to each pupil
Want pupils to be able to respond empathically
Value teaching skills which foster pupil self-expression
Want pupils to be able to think intuitively
Value pupils' free expression work
Wish to broaden pupils' awareness of the world
Want pupils to be able to express their feelings
Value pupils' ideas and questions for assessing creativity

Source: Adapted from Fryer, 1989.

NOVEL FINDINGS

There do not appear to have been any previous reports demonstrating these kinds of intergroup differences in perceptions of creativity. Furthermore, the differences follow a pattern which is consistent with how the teachers prefer to teach – teachers who see creativity in very personal terms prefer a pupil-oriented way of teaching, whilst staff who see creativity in impersonal terms prefer an instrumental approach in their teaching.

Because such findings were not expected, no measure of person orientation was included in the main investigation. However, a measure was included in a later study (Fryer, 1994b). In this, a small representative sample of teachers completed Fryer's Orientation to Creativity Scale, together with Collings's Person Orientation Scale and a measure of learning style. As expected, a moderate to high correlation between orientation to creativity and person orientation was found, but there was no correlation between either of them and the measure of learning style.

In a psychological sense, that is, to make best use of all the various ways in which children learn, both the pupil-oriented and instrumental approaches to teaching are needed. The combination is neither excessively authoritarian nor permissive. Classroom arrangements are not the most critical feature. What is critical is that pupils are deeply and actively involved in learning which is relevant to them and their future needs. This necessarily involves their being highly skilled in thinking for themselves. To achieve this, high quality teaching is needed, using a range of methods and taking account of a complexity of variables.

Such an approach would satisfy the skill requirements of modern, innovative organizations of the kind identified by Helgesen (1990). She argues that what is needed is a balance of efficiency (a traditionally male preoccupation) and humanity (a traditionally female one). Focusing on managers of successful innovative companies, she identifies the requirements as including 'breadth of vision . . . a "diverse portfolio of skills," . . . and the ability to think creatively' (Helgesen, 1990, p. 30). In her experience, women managers have so far been the more successful in combining these. She argues that the traditional male values of independence, autonomy and competition were well suited to old-style, hierarchical organizations which had clear chains of command and communication channels. As both Egan (1992) and Glasser (1992) have argued, traditional 'factory' schooling is no longer appropriate to the needs of modern organizations.

SUMMARY

In Project 1000, male and female staff differ both in the way they prefer to teach and the way they perceive creativity, with females adopting a personal view of creativity and preferring to teach in person-oriented ways, whilst males perceive creativity less personally and prefer to teach in more instrumental ways. When subject specialists are considered, creative arts staff, nurses and general subject teachers also see creativity in personal ways and prefer a pupil-oriented approach to teaching, whereas those teaching maths, science and technology have attitudes and perceptions congruent with those of the male staff. These findings hold good when male and female subject staff are considered separately. The teachers who are most positive about creativity also have a clear preference for pupil-orientation.

All these findings are in line with the results of person orientation research. Indeed, person orientation and orientation to creativity have been found to correlate closely. Full details of these and other intergroup differences are given in Fryer (1989; 1991b; 1994b) and in Fryer and Collings (1991a; 1991b).

6

Teachers' attitudes to pupils' creativity

Teachers can be either the most significant positive factor or the main hindrance.

(female primary teacher)

The intention in this chapter is to explore how the teachers feel about their pupils' creative characteristics.

ATTITUDES TO HIGHLY CREATIVE PUPILS

Not all teachers like highly creative pupils. In a rare, comprehensive study of teachers' views about creativity, Swedish educators expressed ambivalent and negative attitudes towards the pupils they thought were creative. They described them as a worrying element, wanting to do everything differently, unwilling to co-operate, adjusting badly to conventional tuition, troublesome in class, egocentric and egotistical, listless at the prospect of some subjects, cheeky, careless, coming up with strange ideas and disobedient (Eriksson, 1970).

Perhaps this is not too surprising since Cropley reports how hard it is for some highly creative children to cope with school. One boy he cites, by way of illustration, 'had difficulty concentrating, disturbed other children and did poorly in tests . . . his parents were advised that he was suffering from a learning disability', yet psychological testing revealed that this child had an IQ of 170. Cropley suggests that such children do not adjust well to school because they are 'too full of ideas, too demanding, and too excited about the opportunities offered by school' (Cropley, 1992, p. 69).

Another example can be taken from higher education. For instance, a highly creative student often asks such unusual questions that one's initial reaction is that she has not understood, but a moment's thought reveals that she is being really perceptive. In fact she frequently raises some very important issues. When this kind of thing happens often, as is common with such students, it can interrupt the smooth flow of the lesson – something which Torrance and his colleagues have found that teachers generally do not like (Torrance, 1965).

When the Swedish teachers were asked how they would react to pupils' suggestions for an activity that would interrupt the smooth flow of the lesson or lead to unusual questions, their responses were guarded. They felt that unusual questions and suggestions would probably disturb the teachers more than the other children. However, they said they would take into account both the implications for the class and the lesson when deciding what to do, incorporating pupils' suggestions if they fitted in with the lesson or would be useful for the whole class. Some said they would prefer to carry out pupils' suggestions at another time or during a fun hour, but others indicated that they would carry through a pupil's idea, even if the other pupils were less keen (Eriksson, 1970).

CHARACTERISTICS TEACHERS VALUE

Although there have been very few comprehensive studies of teachers' views about creativity, there has been rather more research into their attitudes to creative pupils. Many such studies have employed a personality checklist devised by Torrance and his colleagues, called the 'Ideal Pupil' or 'Ideal Child' checklist, since it is designed for use with either teachers or parents (Torrance, 1965; 1975). It was Torrance's awareness of children's sensitivity to the attitudes of significant others, such as teachers and parents, that prompted him to devise this checklist. Its purpose is not to identify *perfect pupils*, but rather the sort of behaviour teachers (or parents) regard as ideal, with a view to finding out how much they value creative behaviour. This measure has been used in a number of countries and was included by the author in Project 1000. The personality characteristics that Torrance and his colleagues found to be associated with creativity are given in Table 6.1.

Table 6.1 Personality characteristics typically associated with creativity

Courageous in convictions
Curious, searching
Independent in judgement
Independent in thinking
Intuitive
Becoming preoccupied with tasks
Unwilling to accept things on mere say-so
Visionary, idealistic
Willing to take risks

Source: Torrance, 1965, pp. 230–2.

According to Eriksson (1970), the Swedish teachers regard positive teacher attitudes as most important for facilitating creativity and research has shown that when teachers are aware of and interested in creativity, children's scores for creative thinking rise sharply, even if they have had no explicit creativity training (Torrance, 1965).

Torrance's Ideal Pupil checklist was used in Project 1000, as one means of assessing the teachers' attitudes to creative pupils and to compare the attitudes of British teachers with those of staff in other countries. In Project 1000, the checklist was also used (for the first time, as far as is known) to compare attitudes to pupils with the teachers' own self-ratings (see Chapter 7). This was something they really enjoyed doing.

TORRANCE'S STUDY OF TEACHERS' ATTITUDES

In 1965, Torrance conducted a major investigation using this checklist. It involved over a thousand teachers and included staff in the United States, Germany, India, Greece and the Philippines. Tables 6.2 and 6.3 chart the pupil behaviours that teachers in his investigation most want to support and to discourage.

Torrance and his colleagues found that all the cultures sampled had some values which supported creativity and some which were questionable or counter-productive. The United States and German teachers' attitudes were

Table 6.2   The five most favoured pupil characteristics for each cultural group in Torrance's (1965) study

United States	Germany	India	Greece	Philippines
Independent in thinking	Sincere	Curious	Energetic	Industrious
Curious	Sense of humour	Obedient	Strives for distant goals	Obedient
Sense of humour	Industrious	Does work on time	Thorough	Courteous
Considerate of others	Independent in thinking	Courteous	Sincere	Healthy
Industrious	Attempts difficult tasks	Healthy	Non-conforming	Considerate of others

Source: Extract reproduced with the kind permission of the author.

Table 6.3   The five least favoured pupil characteristics for each cultural group in Torrance's (1965) study

United States	Germany	India	Greece	Philippines
Haughty and self-satisfied	Disturbs class	Disturbs class	Haughty and self-satisfied	Stubborn
Domineering	Fault finding	Fault finding	Negativistic	Talkative /Disturbs class
Negativistic	Talkative	Talkative	Timid	Bashful
Disturbs class	Haughty	Regresses	Domineering	Timid
Fault finding	Domineering	Stubborn	Disturbs class	Fault finding

Source: Extract reproduced with the kind permission of the author.

most in line with the ratings of his panel of creativity experts, followed by India, Greece and the Philippines.

Clearly there are cultural differences between countries which have a bearing on the attributes they value and it must be remembered that this study is now thirty years old. However, Torrance concluded that on the basis of the measure, teachers in all five cultures were insufficiently valuing the good guesser, the child who is courageous in convictions, the emotionally sensitive child, the intuitive thinker, children who regress occasionally, those he describes as visionary and those unwilling to accept assertions without evidence. On the other hand, the teachers appeared to be giving pupils unduly great rewards for being courteous, doing work on time, and being obedient, popular and willing to accept the judgements of authorities.

Only the United States teachers unduly discouraged strong emotional feelings and excessively encouraged receptivity to others' ideas. German, Greek and American teachers valued a sense of humour. Both the US and German teachers wanted to encourage versatility, well-roundedness and independence in thinking. Both the US and Greek staff valued talkativeness.

Other investigations in which Torrance's checklist has been used include a small study carried out in New York by Schaefer (1973) and a larger one, carried out by Ohuche (1986) in Nigeria.

Schaefer used the checklist to investigate the attitudes of ten Bronx teachers of emotionally disturbed boys, aged six to fourteen, and eleven Queens teachers working in schools mainly serving disadvantaged children. What the Bronx teachers most wanted for their pupils was that they should wish to excel. Next most important to them was that the children should be curious and self-starters. They ranked fourth, consideration for others, followed by determination and independence in thinking. The teachers from Queens valued social skills and skills which would assist creativity.

Ohuche (1986) points out that, although the Igbos are an ethnic group of about ten million people, there have been very few studies of their creative abilities. Indeed, in Nigeria as a whole, very few studies of creativity appear to have been carried out. Since she regards creativity development as highly relevant to Nigerian education, Ohuche deplores its neglect.

One hundred and twenty-seven secondary teachers took part in her study. Ohuche notes that the Igbo teachers attach a great deal of importance to industry, sincerity, obedience, consideration for others and self-confidence, but not to non-conformity or timidity. They also want to discourage domineering, fault-finding and negativistic behaviour. She comments that it is hardly surprising that Igbo teachers want their pupils to be industrious, since the Nigerian educational system is highly competitive and examination success is highly prized. As elsewhere, examinations tend to emphasize critical thinking.

Ohuche describes the Igbo culture as valuing conformity. In this respect it has a great deal in common with many other cultures. The opposite extreme can simply result in chaos. To encourage creativity, a balanced education is required (Fryer, 1989; 1993; Cropley, 1992).

THE BRITISH TEACHERS' ATTITUDES

As far as the British teachers are concerned, the five characteristics they most value are given in Table 6.4 and the five they least value in Table 6.5. A complete list of results is available in Fryer (1989).

In Project 1000, no single characteristic was selected for particular encouragement by even half the sample. The two most highly rated

Table 6.4 The five characteristics from the Torrance Ideal Pupil Checklist most often selected by the Project 1000 teachers as worthy of special encouragement (N = 1028) (%)

Characteristic	Worth special encouragement
Considerate	45
Socially well-adjusted	29
Self-confident	27
Independent in thinking	24
Curious	20

Source: Adapted from Fryer, 1989.

Table 6.5 The five characteristics from the Torrance Ideal Pupil Checklist most often selected by the Project 1000 teachers as needing to be discouraged (N = 1028) (%)

Characteristic	To be discouraged
Negativistic	62
Haughty and self-satisfied	48
Stubborn and obstinate	48
Disturbing group organization and procedures	45
Domineering	44

Source: Adapted from Fryer, 1989.

characteristics each involve social skills – 'considerate of others' and 'socially well-adjusted'. However, the three next most popular choices do reflect a willingness to support creativity – 'self-confidence', 'independence in thinking' and 'curiosity' – even though less than a third of the teachers have singled these out for special encouragement. 'Self-confidence' was not included in the top five choices of any country in Torrance's 1965 study, but was selected by the Igbo teachers in Ohuche's Nigerian investigation.

As Table 6.5 indicates, there is more agreement amongst the UK teachers about characteristics they want to discourage. The results are consistent with Torrance's findings. These characteristics may sound undesirable but, as

Young (1982) reminds us, creativity implies the negative just as much as the positive. Often what has gone before gets swept away. 'Creating is tearing down as well as building up' (Young, 1982, p. 262). The destructive aspects of creativity are not always acknowledged. A pupil who is apt to disagree with the majority may well be perceived unfavourably, even if such dissension is valid, useful or both. Most scientific progress has involved questioning the accepted view (von Oech, 1990; and others).

'Disturbing the group's organization and procedures' is fairly typical of creative pupils, according to Torrance and his colleagues. Half the British teachers want to discourage this, as did the teachers in Torrance's 1965 study. This is entirely understandable given the pressures on staff. Despite this, the British teachers do seem more willing to encourage creativity than those involved in earlier studies. A Project 1000 teacher working with children with hearing difficulties said 'I try to be a creative teacher; I would like to be one. My goal for the children is self-sufficiency'.

Indeed, many of the British teachers are willing to support their pupils' creativity even though it is not easy to do so, faced as they are, with overlarge classes, inadequate time to prepare lessons, burgeoning administrative duties and inadequate resources. In fact, as we shall see in the next chapter, they are more willing to encourage creativity in their pupils than to recognize it in themselves.

SUMMARY

Although there have not been many studies of teachers' views about creativity in general, there have been a number employing the Torrance checklists to ascertain teachers' attitudes to creative behaviour. In a major international investigation, Torrance found that teachers generally attach too much importance to characteristics which make pupils easy to teach, but undervalue many typically creative attributes such as guessing/hypothesizing, being courageous in convictions, intuitive thinking and unwillingness to accept assertions without evidence. However, the British teachers appear to be rather more willing to support creative behaviour.

7

Teachers as facilitators of creativity

To teach is to learn twice over.
(Joseph Joubert, *Pensees*, 1842)

HOW TEACHERS SEE THEMSELVES

Torrance and Myers (1970) maintain that few professions can be regarded as more creative than teaching, yet hardly any of the teachers involved in their research project saw themselves as creative. The Romanian teachers studied by Popescu-Nevianu and Cretsu (1986) said that they did not value initiative in themselves, but they valued it highly in others. They tended to be modest and have a low self-image. They did not like to take risks for the sake of innovation and preferred to stick with the teaching style to which they were accustomed. However they did recognize the importance of the teacher being creative for successful creativity development in children. Since then, it has been my good fortune to meet some very creative Romanian teachers.

In Chapter 6 we saw how the 'Ideal Pupil' checklist (Torrance, 1965; 1975) was used to find out whether teachers want to support their pupils' creative behaviour. To find out how teachers see themselves, a virtually identical 'Personality' checklist (also devised by Torrance, 1975) was used. Prior to Project 1000, these two checklists do not appear to have been used together in the same investigation. They provide a neat way of assessing how closely teachers' self-perceptions match the pupil characteristics they want to support.

The teachers had to select five attributes which they thought best described themselves, as well as five with which they least identified (Tables 7.1 and 7.2). Interestingly, no single category was selected by more than half the sample.

What is also striking is that only a small proportion of teachers identify with the nine characteristics identified by Torrance's panel of experts as most typical of creative people (see Table 7.3 – the percentage of British teachers identifying with each characteristic is given alongside the characteristic in question). Instead, the teachers perceive themselves mainly in terms of their social attributes and willingness to work hard (see Table 7.1). Hardly any of them identify with 'quiet'! It is also worth noting that curiosity and independence in thinking are the only attributes listed in Table 7.3 that the Project 1000 teachers wish to especially encourage in their pupils (see Table

Table 7.1   The five characteristics on the Torrance Personality Checklist which the Project 1000 teachers most frequently identified as 'most like them' (N = 1028) (%)

Characteristic	Most like me
Sense of humour	36
Considerate	28
Emotionally sensitive	20
Industrious, busy	19
Affectionate	16

Source: Adapted from Fryer, 1989.

Table 7.2   The five characteristics on the Torrance Personality Checklist which the Project 1000 teachers most frequently identified as 'least like them' (N = 1028) (%)

Characteristic	Least like me
Haughty, self-satisfied	46
Negativistic	34
Timid, shy, bashful	33
Domineering	26
Quiet	22

Source: Adapted from Fryer, 1989.

6.4, Chapter 6). The full results on which Tables 7.1 to 7.3 are based can be found in Fryer (1989).

On the basis of these findings it seems that the British teachers do not, as a group, see themselves as creative, yet almost all of them (94 per cent) feel that if the teacher is creative it helps children to develop their creativity.

TEACHERS LEAST, MODERATELY AND MOST POSITIVE ABOUT CREATIVITY

As reported in Chapter 5, three subgroups were identified – comprising teachers least, moderately and most oriented to creativity. As we have seen, those in the most keen group (17 per cent) were found to be significantly more 'pupil oriented' than those in the least keen group (9 per cent). A description of 'pupil orientation' is given in Chapter 5. From the statistical analysis as a whole and from later research work it has been possible to devise a robust 'Orientation to Creativity' scale (Fryer, 1989; 1993; 1994b).

It is perhaps worth noting that, when four of the teachers in the least keen group were interviewed, they said they envisaged creativity as a rare gift,

Table 7.3 Percentage of Project 1000 teachers who most identify with typically creative characteristics from Torrance's Personality Checklist (N = 1028)

Characteristic	%
Courageous in convictions	5.4
Curious, searching	7.8
Independent in judgement	5.4
Independent in thinking	12.5
Intuitive	12.1
Becoming preoccupied with tasks	6.0
Unwilling to accept things on mere say-so	9.8
Visionary, idealistic	5.0
Willing to take risks	6.8

Source: Adapted from Fryer, 1989.

mainly the province of highly intelligent children and heavily influenced by home background. Of course, this is a small number.

What two teachers, one moderately and one very interested in creativity, have to say about their work is given in rather more detail below. This is not because their views are more important than those of other staff. It is simply that one aim of this book is to provide insights into what teachers think helps develop creativity. If you want to study jumping behaviour, you don't just study people to see how high they happen to jump. You find people who jump and learn from them (Torrance, 1988). In the interests of confidentiality, the names of the teachers profiled below have been changed.

A teacher moderately positive about creativity

Andy is head of chemistry at a comprehensive high school in the north of England. He prefers to use interactive teaching materials, in which his pupils 'get really absorbed'. He likes to set up a non-directive environment where the emphasis is on learning rather than teaching, because it is very important to him that his students can find things out for themselves.

His experience of teaching has led him to the conclusion that children enjoy their work when they can see a purpose in it and want to do it. So for him the key is 'finding the purpose and switching on the want with rewards'. This teacher is not only skilled in reflecting on his own teaching, but also in actively finding out what works for other staff which he can then apply to his own chemistry teaching.

He has found that art, dance and physical education are the most fruitful sources of ideas. From observing these classes, Andy has identified two elements which seem to be making learning both productive and enjoyable. One is 'ownership . . . in art, for example, children get really involved, because it's their picture, they're responsible for every brush stroke'. The other element involves 'knowing that what you are doing is going to take you to some useful end point'. So he believes it is important to make clear to children the purpose of their learning activities.

Andy finds that projects in which pupils can see direct practical benefits from learning are the most motivating (see also Glasser, 1992; 1993). Andy has found his approach particularly successful in getting children of low ability and those with behavioural difficulties involved in science:

> I find some of the really difficult children who might otherwise be away, turn up for science. It's noisy and their notebooks are not wonderfully kept, but in terms of enjoyment and participation it's good. I don't think you can be creative unless you involve yourself and are enjoying yourself.

When he has set up the learning situation, he allows his pupils to assume ownership of the activity, but he does not find it easy to let go. He notes that 'It needs quite a bit of experience to walk away. The temptation is to get stuck in and carry on with them. It's all to do with ownership and what you want to find out'.

Andy would like to see more learning materials available, ones which are flexible enough to enable teachers to adapt them to their own needs, because he thinks that ownership is just as important a part of teachers' motivation as of children's.

Asked what he regards as counter-productive to creativity, Andy says 'A rigid timetable, a formal syllabus, denying pupils autonomy, failing to reward them, setting inappropriate work and providing unattractive textbooks'.

A teacher most positive about creativity

When the data was being collected, the head of a West Country high school said he thought the high schools could learn a lot from primary teachers about how to develop creativity. An interview with a primary teacher from this group follows.

Lesley teaches juniors in a small, Church of England primary school in a Yorkshire town. The school is quite old and traditional in style. Even before the interview began, Lesley said quite spontaneously:

> I think it's difficult, especially with young children, to stop them being creative. I think some people do eventually, but I think very young children are naturally creative. When they come out of the system at the other end, many children – unless they're very strong personalities – have been robbed of it. That sounds like a huge generalization, but it's just my impression.

Lesley says she did her teacher training when 'creativity was all the rage' and the progressive education movement was gaining ground in Britain in the 1960s. Since I was a primary teacher at that time and remembered a lot of silly practices being implemented, mistakenly in the name of progressive education, which were counter-productive to creativity, I was interested to hear why she thought this movement failed. Her answer was, 'Because it went too far – as so often happens in education when things become fashionable. Everyone wanted to jump on the bandwagon – like children, who having been taught to use question marks, then put one at the end of every sentence'. She went on to say that the progressive education movement began to fail when employers realized that young people lacked basic skills. She thinks it would have been better if teachers had taught these whilst at the same time allowing children 'to be'. What is needed in education, she believes, is balance. This is the maxim by which she teaches. She wants her pupils to have both rational and intuitive thinking skills (her terminology) as well as a mastery of basic skills.

She believes it is really important for pupils to find things out for themselves. In an attempt to fit her teaching to each child, she tries to teach in lots of different ways in the hope of catering for a whole variety of children's needs. What she does stress is that she really values every child's contribution. She likes the children to put forward their views and build on one another's ideas, 'If there is a problem to be solved, twenty-seven minds can be brought to bear on it'.

Like Torrance (1984) and Weisberg (1993), Lesley believes that all children should have a mentor, 'an adult mind in tune with their mind that could encourage, foster, enrich, give them experiences and lead them forward'. She recognizes the powerful influence teachers have, 'If the teacher isn't understanding of the creative process and isn't encouraging, then children who want to please the teacher can have that part of themselves destroyed'.

Lesley thinks that to develop creativity, the teacher must care about it and have a feeling for it. This, she believes, is particularly important with primary age children. Unfortunately, she finds that, all too often, children receive messages like 'What are you messing about with that for?' or 'Haven't you finished yet?' whereas what children need is time to mull things over. But she thinks that some teachers wouldn't like that, because it might look as if they weren't doing anything.

She feels that timetabling can also be inhibiting as it can prevent children from 'going to the limits of their thinking'. She would prefer a flexible approach. Another primary teacher, Kernig, has made the same point. She thinks that regimented lesson times encourage shallow learning. Children know that if they get really absorbed in their work, the lesson bell will soon put an end to it (TES, 1985). As we have seen earlier in the book, there appears to be a strong association between enabling children to get deeply involved in their learning and creative productivity. Entwistle (1987) has stressed the educational value of this.

Lesley suggests that the development of creativity is greatly helped by the whole school being involved, with the headteacher's support being especially valuable. This has been mentioned by other staff too. On the other hand, she thinks that inappropriate attitudes on the part of adults are most inhibiting. Related to this, she believes, is a strong emphasis on producing an end product to go on the wall, instead of the teacher being concerned with the process of learning, that is to say, what the children are actually thinking. This point was also mentioned by a Belfast primary teacher (see page 104).

Lesley finds that parents' attitudes can sometimes be inhibiting. Most of the parents of children in her class are excessively anxious for their children to do well. When such anxiety is transferred to the children, it becomes a real block to their creativity, because it makes them afraid to make mistakes – something she believes is exacerbated by an excessive emphasis on testing.

Lesley's work has also been affected by cuts in caretaking hours at her school. Caretaking staff have less time to clean the classrooms, so any messy activities, such as working with clay, are discouraged. She feels under pressure to inhibit practical activities and experimentation.

Lesley feels that the time she spends working with children on an individual basis is particularly valuable. She wishes she could have a regular fifteen minute block of time with each child, since this would enable a great deal of progress to be made. Unfortunately, she finds that such opportunities are rare. However, as she points out, the provision of a non-teaching assistant in every classroom would enable teachers to spend more time working individually, thus making a significant difference to each child's progress. Her frustration at not being able to spend time with individuals is evident from the following remarks:

> I don't always do what I should. It's all very fraught. There's a part of me saying I want this child to follow her train of thought through and another part aware of the constraints and the other children around . . . . I just think children suffer so much from not having individual attention. Others will argue they've got to learn not to have it. They're in the world and it's tough and we mustn't be soft with them. But I keep seeing my role as nurturing . . . and if I've got to keep saying sit down and shut up, I haven't got time for you, then I can't do my job.

FACILITATING CREATIVITY

Sidney Parnes, co-founder of the Creative Education Foundation and himself a most skilled facilitator of creativity, identifies the qualities and skills which facilitators of creativity need (Parnes, 1985). He also provides an excellent account of how to run a creative problem solving session (see Chapter 9). His account clearly illustrates the high level of skill and alertness which facilitators need. This contrasts markedly with *laissez-faire* approaches to teaching.

The intention here is not to repeat Parnes' guidelines, but rather to draw attention to the kinds of skills and qualities he identifies as indicative of good facilitators (and therefore good teachers). These may be categorized into three main areas – skills which are appropriate to group work in general, personal qualities which make a good facilitator *per se*, and cognitive skills which maximize the likelihood of creative outcomes. Inevitably there is some overlap between the categories.

Group work skills

The skills needed for effective group work have much in common with Carl Rogers' approach to teaching and learning (Rogers, 1983). The facilitator also needs the ability to pace a lesson. Good group work involves things like being positive and accepting, respecting everyone's potential for creativity, being able to draw out ideas from people and being tactful. It involves being good at building a productive group, being able to monitor the group's non-verbal signals and managing the process in terms of time constraints, whilst maintaining flexibility within these. Facilitators must make the process enjoyable and should be prepared to allow some foolish behaviour, whilst striving towards a serious goal. They must not force their own ideas on the group.

Personal qualities

Facilitators should be sincerely enthusiastic, dedicated, optimistic, flexible and spontaneous. They should not take themselves too seriously and, importantly, not feel they need to be in the limelight.

Cognitive characteristics

Facilitators need to be wide categorizers and open to ideas (see also Chapter 3; Cropley, 1967). They should invite ambiguity but maintain the balance necessary to bring a greater order from the disorder of ambiguity; and be ready to take calculated risks. (Parnes is talking about disorder and risk in terms of ideas, not behaviour).

Hopefully, these categories give a flavour of Parnes' approach, but they are no substitute for his text or for seeing him in action, skilfully exemplifying his own recommendations.

MENTORS AND CREATIVITY

One of Lesley's suggestions was that every child should have a mentor. This does not have to be the teacher. Many schools make use of the wealth of knowledge and skills in the community. Mentors can be recruited as volunteers. Torrance provides evidence from a twenty-two-year longitudinal study that the presence or absence of a mentor can make a difference to mentees' creative achievements and educational attainments in adulthood that cannot be explained by chance.

Torrance describes mentors as older persons who share mentees' educational experience [in some way] and take them under their wing. He describes the relationship as one of 'depth and caring' (Torrance, 1984, p. 2). This text is useful in that it explores the various kinds of issues in mentor/mentee relationships and it documents how young people without mentors fare.

Torrance cites several examples of individuals who have suffered because they lacked a mentor, especially young people who were unaware that they were creative. One example is a girl living in a deprived area who achieved really high scores on both *intelligence* and *creativity* tests in first grade (my italics). Whilst ignoring her distinct abilities, her parents, teacher and school social worker concerned themselves with ridding this six-year-old of her imaginary playmates. Torrance describes how her work deteriorated and eventually she dropped out of school. Worse still, in adulthood she did not perceive herself as very clever, though she said she hoped to finish high school one day and maybe go into nursing. Torrance comments that things might have turned out very differently for her if she had been assigned a mentor instead of a social worker to help rid her of her imaginary playmates. This is a particularly sad account in view of the role imagination plays in human cognition, as discussed in Chapter 4.

Torrance sees the mentor's role as encouraging and supporting the mentee in expressing and testing ideas and thinking things through. He suggests that this includes protecting the mentee from peer and superior reactions until his or her ideas have been tested and modified. Torrance does of course point out that mentor relationships can fail for a number of reasons. For example, the mentor may be too limited in perspective and not a good competence model. Also, various differences between the mentor and mentee can prevent them from establishing the essential rapport. Barry Fryer (1994) highlights problems with mentoring based on UK experience, including mentors failing to understand their mentoring role, not understanding the learning processes they are supposed to nurture, and simply failing to find the time to perform their mentoring properly.

Torrance has devised a set of guidelines for mentors which includes helping their mentees become immersed in something and 'pursue it with intensity and depth', capitalize on their strengths in pursuit of their dreams, whilst freeing themselves from others' expectations, and avoiding 'wasting a lot of expensive unproductive energy in trying to be well-rounded'. He suggests that mentees should be encouraged to 'find some great teachers and attach themselves to these teachers' (Torrance, 1984, pp. 56–7).

SCHOOL ETHOS

Whole school commitment

The Project 1000 teachers who expressed an interest in developing creativity recognized the value of the whole school, or at least a whole department, being committed to it. For example, a head of science expressed concern that without this broad commitment, pupils might mistakenly think that those teachers who were committed to creativity were demanding less of them, when in fact they were demanding more. He suggested that a formal mechanism for the exchange of ideas about creativity development among staff would increase the uptake of such an approach. Generally ideas only circulated on an *ad hoc* basis in his school.

The importance of the headteacher's support

Like Lesley, just about all the other teachers think the headteacher's attitude is crucial. The head's support means a great deal to them. This is especially the case in schools where staff interested in developing creativity are in the minority. A science teacher, working in an inner-city middle school, said her headteacher was the only other person in the school who shared her enthusiasm. This gave her confidence to continue. Stein (1994b) highlights the crucial role played by intermediaries (such as headteachers) in supporting creativity.

The relationship between teachers and pupils

Teachers have a key role to play in the development of their pupils' creativity (Torrance and Myers, 1970). Ochse (1990) cites countless examples of teachers singled out for praise by their former pupils, because they made a real difference to their pupils' success. One noteworthy example is Einstein who praised his teacher, Reuss, for being more flexible and less conforming than the other teachers and for encouraging students to be independent thinkers.

In Project 1000, a head of art and design at a West Country high school commented, 'Teaching has to be like personal relationships – you can't insist on attitudes. You can be nice to pupils and hope they will respond to you'.

He went on to say that if you want pupils to be creative, you have to persuade them they can be. He does not believe you can direct students to be creative. It is more a case of creating the right kind of environment for creativity to happen. This teacher said he thought pressure very rarely resulted in the production of creative work. Mock (1970) has also observed how the teacher's personality can have a significant impact on students' imagination. At the same time she rejects a *laissez-faire* approach to teaching.

A college tutor felt it was unrealistic to expect to build a rewarding tutor/student relationship with every student. However, she did try to protect them from institutional goals, when she felt they conflicted with her students' best interests:

> I've learned not to get too involved because you can't carry everything. You can't win every student. I don't really want to do that. I wouldn't find that very fulfilling. We are under pressure to get students on to higher courses, but I don't want to be a sausage machine. I have to see a student as an individual. But I get repercussions from higher management if I encourage students to go for what they want, instead of aiming for the highest courses possible.

Many staff are all too aware that, for some children, being in school is the most stable and tranquil part of their lives:

> There should be somewhere, and school has to be the place where they're encouraged to be themselves. If they go home and it's awful, there's someone who will listen to them. They've got to feel they can trust you. But if everyone they've ever encountered has made them feel worthless or useless – at least they can say their teachers value them.

Another teacher felt that school is a place 'where children feel safe, wanted and valued by one another and the adults working there. Safety is something people neglect in school. Some children don't feel safe there, because they've been bullied or the teacher picks on them'.

Teachers' self confidence

Naturally how teachers feel about themselves has a distinct bearing on their pupils, as one teacher points out

> It is the confident teacher/adult who allows the child to be confident within the task. The adult may inhibit further thinking and creativity . . . by defining the horizon . . . . The child learns what is difficult from the adult . . . so adults must not impose their own limitations.

One of the characteristics of creative people is risk-taking (Cropley, 1967). A similar idea is expressed by a social care lecturer:

> I think education is about taking risks and sometimes things will fall apart, but if you're not prepared to take risks which might result in failure, then you won't get the kind of results the group is capable of. A lot of the time I believe in going out and trying, to see what happens. I occasionally fall on my face, but I think humility is an important characteristic in creative teaching. You say you're sorry and get on with the job. If you're concerned about looking good and close it down, that's a shame. If you can continue with an uncomfortable, difficult situation, some good can come out of it.

SUMMARY

Teaching is a most creative profession, yet few staff think they are creative. Instead, they describe themselves in terms of their social attributes. Teachers representing the groups least, moderately and most keen on developing creativity describe themselves differently and they differ in what they have to say about pupils and how they prefer to teach them.

Teachers representing the least keen group see creativity development as something over which they have little influence. The teacher who represents the most keen group believes that working individually with a child on a regular basis (if only for a short time) would make a significant difference to the child's performance. The provision of classroom assistants could help with this. It is worth noting that this teacher also values a balanced approach to education. Her perception of creativity encompasses both the personal perspective typical of female teachers and the object-oriented perspective, more typical of male teachers.

This teacher also believes that each child would benefit from having a mentor, who could be a suitable volunteer from the local community. The value of a mentor has been stressed by Torrance, who also emphasizes the importance of allowing children to get deeply involved in work which interests them. Parnes's guidelines for facilitators of creativity are to be recommended.

8

Teachers developing creativity

'Do you know what A means, little Piglet?'
'No, Eeyore, I don't'.
'It means Learning, it means Education, it means all the things that you and Pooh haven't got. That's what A means.' . . . . 'I'm telling you. People come and go in this Forest . . . They walk to and fro saying, "Ha ha!". But do they know anything about A? They don't. It's just three sticks to *them*.'
(A. A. Milne, *The House at Pooh Corner*, p. 85, 1986)

This chapter recounts what the Project 1000 teachers have to say about developing creativity in schools and colleges. The teachers recognize the need to integrate the numerous factors involved in promoting creativity in students. They have many sound ideas which others may find helpful.

WHAT TEACHERS THINK ABOUT THE DEVELOPMENT OF CREATIVITY

Almost all the teachers think that creativity can be developed. Most of them (94 per cent) see teachers as having a central role to play in developing children's and young people's creativity. When asked how this might be achieved, all of them talked about the conditions they saw as supportive and the styles and strategies they regarded as relevant. Hardly any of them referred to teaching problem solving. As one teacher put it:

> You can't teach creativity but you can facilitate it. You provide resources and teach skills. Basically it's a question of negotiation and allowing children adequate access to opportunities and experience, without a disorganized riot. It's 'directive opportunism' for the children. But you've got to have a programme of skills, concepts, attitudes – with evaluation methods built in.

A similar sentiment was expressed by a high school English teacher who felt that 'creativity cannot always be taught by a teacher, but it can be encouraged and developed to a very high level'.

Table 8.1 identifies the factors the whole group of Project 1000 teachers regard as supportive of creativity development and Table 8.2 summarizes what those who also took part in interviews had to say (some of this is recounted below). Also relevant are the views of the two staff profiled in Chapter 7, who represent the groups who are 'moderately' and 'extremely' positive about creativity.

Table 8.1 The twelve factors which Project 1000 teachers think most assist the development of creativity (N = 922)

Characteristic	% of teachers who think it helps
Building pupils' confidence	99
Encouraging pupils to ask questions	97
A creative teacher	94
Some free choice at home	92
Some choice of tasks	90
Involved and supportive family	89
Some choice of learning methods	75
Informal teaching	70
Asking provocative questions	68
Setting some unassessed tasks	64
Emphasizing success	60
Setting goals/making expectations clear	54

Source: Adapted from Fryer, 1989.

Approaches to teaching, learning and developing creativity

A West Country teacher-librarian describes how she sees creativity fitting into her day-to-day teaching:

> You have to be quite nurturing. But having said that, it only happens in between rushing from one lesson to another and all the physical problems about getting things sorted and organized. I think you have to be quite organized about being 'loose'. It's something to do with classroom management . . . the relationship between you and the kids and . . . the sense of value.

It is evident from what this teacher says that she does not regard unstructured or *laissez-faire* approaches as especially helpful in developing creativity. This is in keeping with the views of Torrance and Myers (1970) who argue that much more is needed than a permissive environment. They maintain that teaching creatively demands commitment and involvement, guidance and direction

Table 8.2 Factors the teachers who were interviewed think would help in the development of creativity (N = 31)

Category	%
Affective/personality	
valuing creativity, building confidence, giving permission for creativity, encouraging trust, pupil personality characteristics – self-confidence and willingness to 'attack', encouraging expression of feelings, praise, being interested.	61.3
Cognitive/task	
providing a mentor, one to one teaching, encouraging questions, encouraging risk-taking, developing skills, developing critical faculties, balanced teaching, active learning, practical work, encouraging problem solving, knowing when to stand back and do nothing.	90.0
Cognitive/affective	
negotiating learning, allowing autonomy, removing pressure, positively fostering creativity, teaching self-evaluation, letting pupils express ideas.	38.7
Environmental	
a safe, friendly environment, favourable or unfavourable conditions, no special conditions, adverse conditions, bad experiences, opportunities for creativity, flexible environment.	29.0
Cognitive/environmental	
providing interesting work, providing firsthand experience.	19.4

Source: Adapted from Fryer, 1989.

which is both sensitive and aware, intent listening, protecting pupils against disparagement and ridicule and recognizing real efforts as sufficiently worthwhile to encourage further effort.

Although three-quarters of the staff surveyed think that teaching informally does contribute to pupils' creativity, at least half of the 1028 teachers do not equate informality with permissiveness.

Among the staff interviewed, all shades of opinion are to be found. For example a primary teacher said:

I think children finding things out for themselves is very important. In the play area, we give them time to make discoveries and find out things. They're not hassled and told to go and do things. They're allowed to pick what they want and have time to enjoy it and talk with their friends about it – not having the teacher breathing down their necks, bombarding them with questions. If children don't know what they want to do, I don't think they should be forced. I try and find an area which interests them.

A high school drama teacher recommends that more staff should 'move away from the didactic chalk and talk approach'. She suggests that some staff, particularly older ones, rely excessively on formal teaching. She attributes this partly to their ignorance of other teaching methods and partly to insecurities about using such methods.

However, the teacher is at pains to point out that she is not advocating 'children running riot', but rather 'negotiated learning' in which it is not just the teacher who generates ideas. This teacher has carried out a number of small surveys, which reveal that twelve- and thirteen-year-olds spend 75 per cent of their time just writing. Half the remaining time they spend listening to the teacher 'so there is very little time left for them to learn in other ways'.

Many of the teachers (83 per cent) think that a constrained environment is counter-productive to creativity. One reason they give is that they cannot see how it can be flexible enough to meet every child's learning needs. At the same time there are those who feel that the quality of informal teaching is not guaranteed either. This depends on the skill of each individual teacher. As a deputy head points out 'You might think informal teaching would stimulate creativity, and it can do so, but it can also be so lacking in guidance and stimulation that it can be stifling'.

Some teachers argue for a balanced approach, for example:

My view of education is as a creative process, bringing out the best in people. If you're working towards a product, some organization helps. A permissive atmosphere both helps and hinders; I think you need a happy medium. If you give people freedom, you can get a situation where creativity will occur, but things can get out of hand. If the group is totally free, some group members will dominate others and prevent them expressing their viewpoint – so a happy medium [is needed], but this can vary from day to day and group to group.

An infant teacher pointed out that teachers can't just act as 'resource providers' – allowing young children to do their own thing. Teachers have to provide lots of different kinds of stimulating materials and firsthand experiences. They have to gain children's interest from the outset, perhaps with something they have brought in to school, such as a piece of music.

Management writer, Saul Gellerman (1979), made a useful analogy between management education and farming. Like the farmer, the teacher controls some of the variables but has to hope that nature will co-operate with the others. Using a similar analogy, a primary teacher likens teaching to gardening:

In teaching, I think you have to sow the seeds and watch them grow. You give the children as many opportunities as possible to be creative. It takes a stimulating environment, a good teacher, a friendly atmosphere, a chance to mix with peers, to discuss and do things – a chance to get outside the narrow confines of their lives, even if it's just via a story.

Another teacher recognized that creativity did not just happen: 'Children's creativity has to spring from somewhere. You have to till the ground and prepare it. Some children need this more than others, especially urban children who don't get beyond the end of the street or the TV set – often not beyond the front door'. This has also been stressed by Ogilvie (1974) who points out that creativity cannot arise from nothing. In similar vein, Mock argues that teachers should not be afraid to teach skills, but at the same time children should be prepared for working on their own initiative.

Torrance and Myers point out that, whilst the ideal relationship between pupil and teacher should be non-threatening, it is not possible to be too prescriptive about teaching styles, as teachers need to find out what suits them best. Gray and Satterly (1981) suggest that any decisions about teaching effectiveness need to take account of a whole range of variables such as the quality of classroom discussions and the extent to which pupils' capabilities match what their teachers provide. Perhaps the last word on this should go to the primary teacher who said:

> It is necessary to 'like' children and take an interest in them. They will respond to that. Too often I believe education is a process of superimposing a set of wonderful ideas devised by earnest educationalists upon a set of small people. That cannot be right.

Some of the teachers interviewed think that some structure is important, since you can't just tell children to be creative and expect them to get on with it. One of the teachers felt that tasks have to be defined quite tightly. Children need 'stepping stones, building something up in little parts, which can be brought together and then hopefully the child can take off'. Such an approach may suit children with *serialist* learning styles, who like to master one area in detail before going on to another; but it may not suit *holists* so well, those who learn best by mastering the overall picture before filling in the details (Pask and Scott, 1972). Pask (1976) has found that the mismatching of serialist and holist teaching and learning styles inhibits pupils' performance.

Several teachers said they took children's anxiety levels into account. Those who did all thought that tightly structured work could provide anxious children with a sense of security, whereas more confident pupils could cope with greater freedom. A junior year head said she thought that all children feel happier with a structure to follow, but it is important that they should understand that it can be modified.

A high school design technology teacher who describes creativity as 'lots of different ways of solving a problem and actually doing it', says that his teaching style is sometimes traditional, sometimes liberal. He finds that many children cannot handle an informal system and have tremendous difficulty coping with responsibility. He attributes this to their home experiences, but wants them to be able to show initiative:

> Some children either have extreme freedom at home or no interest is shown in them. In other cases, parents are so heavy-handed that children can't cope when they're not being told what to do . . . . I think we've got to get kids to do things that require initiative. This is what life needs and it's character building. Such activities require lots of planning to be successful.

The curriculum

The deputy head of a junior school maintains that 'The curriculum must allow creativity in children – allowing them to explore, invent and develop'. Not all staff share this broad definition of creativity, however. There was a pervasive view that creativity is only relevant to the arts, albeit across the whole spectrum. One teacher commented: 'In educational terms you have to develop creativity on a broad front – in all the expressive and creative arts, not just one. It has to be a continuous process – not just art on Thursdays'.

WHAT TEACHERS THINK PROMOTES CREATIVITY

Setting interesting tasks

Teachers can act as catalysts, devising tasks which fire children's enthusiasm. This is the opinion of a Merseyside art and design teacher:

In art, we can be very devious in putting things before children to act as a catalyst. That's our skill. We're having an arts festival project 'The Land and The Sea', in collaboration with another department. The kids have taken off! That's when you get the real high in teaching – when you get kids begging to come out of other lessons. They desperately want to have their work shown. They're not just copying or doing things they've been told. They want to do certain things and seek the teacher's help in doing them. I actually enjoy teaching and I like being with kids . . . . I'm sure if I'm enjoying it, the kids are too.

A further education lecturer recalls her experience of what happens in secondary school when teachers lack this enthusiasm. In the beginning, the pupils 'always seem fairly optimistic, but by the second year [they begin to lose interest] if they've not been encouraged to find themselves and take responsibility for themselves . . . by the fourth form it's horrendous if they haven't been encouraged'.

Teaching skills

Mock (1970) maintains that teachers should not be afraid to teach skills. She is concerned that many young children receive no guidance about how to use materials, because of a faulty impression that this will in some way damage their spontaneous imagination. All the evidence about creativity development supports her view.

An infant teacher in Project 1000 feels that, although ideas may come from the children, there has to be a certain amount of suggestion. Children need to be shown how things can develop. This teacher stresses that she is not suggesting 'stamping on the children', but simply making them aware of different ways of doing things.

This is how a primary school head describes her approach:

My teaching style involves education for the children – starting from what they know and building it up, stretching the children and pushing them into other arts and science areas – the whole spectrum. I try to pay most attention to the areas where I am weak personally. There is a danger in over-developing children in areas where you are brilliant and ignoring the rest. Breadth and balance are crucial.

Using music and drama

A primary teacher explains 'The most exciting and interesting results I have achieved in primary school have been through music, which in certain cases has a calming effect on children, leading them to be thoughtful, ask questions and perform much better. This stimulates growth in other subject areas'.

Educational drama is thought to provide children with both the opportunity to grow in confidence and to develop the problem solving skills they need to be creative:

By its nature drama is creative, if properly taught. Children can use their imagination and be naturally creative. Children must be active, not passive. Creativity isn't the main aim, but rather children's social development . . . . Drama develops confidence all round. There are children who would not contribute to a group situation, but drama has helped them.

I think pupils should be involved in decision-making. Creativity comes out of being responsible for part of one's own learning, which involves making decisions . . . . Decision-making is very much part of educational drama . . . . I don't feel children will learn anything if I just go in and say 'Right, today we're going to do something about deserts'. I'd much rather discuss, letting the children make decisions. I will advise, co-ordinate – whatever the children need.

Educational drama is going towards creativity and child development. Being a good actor doesn't make a child creative. If children are confident, show imagination and originality of thought and can make decisions then children are being creative, even if they are not academically able.

(English and drama teacher)

Encouraging questions

Almost all the teachers think that encouraging pupils to ask questions is a key aspect of creativity development, as does Torrance (1965). Unfortunately, pupils' questions are not encouraged as much as they might be. Instead, much classroom talk is teacher-directed (Young, 1984). Young is concerned that, unless teachers are very careful, classroom discussion can degenerate towards indoctrination, if teachers selectively attend to those ideas and questions which support their own arguments and ignore or dismiss those which do not.

Providing firsthand experiences

Several infant and junior teachers highlighted the importance of children having firsthand experiences of the real world. Certain infant teachers expressed the view that young children are naturally creative, so all that teachers have to do is add training in basic skills. But some of those teaching older juniors felt that they also have to try and fill significant gaps in children's firsthand experiences – as in the case of an inner-city child, who found a school outing to the countryside a frightening experience, because he had only ever been to the countryside twice. He was nine years old. Dealing with this kind of problem requires a lot of productive thinking on the part of staff, according to a head of infants, who also remarked:

> To develop creativity, children's imagination has to be fired. For instance, we had a clown workshop and the materials you provide helps – water and sand, plain and coloured, water with bubbles . . . . Schools ought to be full of experiences which fire the imagination. Lots of infants have been to the park this week. Once they've actually seen, say, a squirrel, their collage or whatever they're doing is that much better. And once they've seen the quality of what they can achieve, then that inspires them to improve the quality of a lot of other things. So the more you can take them out – the more good educational experiences you can provide – the more it helps.

A maths specialist described how children can use firsthand materials to get answers to problems. It also helps them realize that there is more than one route to a solution. Mock (1970, p. 94) stresses the role of firsthand experiences in the development of imaginative thinking, but she emphasizes the importance of allowing children to experience things in their own way – like the child who described a visit to Caernarfon Castle as 'the day we saw the dead dog by the roadside'.

Giving some choice

The teacher-librarian quoted at the beginning of this chapter said she thought that if children are given choice, their attitude to a piece of work will be more creative:

> You have to be committed to a piece of work to allow creativity to take place . . . . I feel certain parameters have to be defined, such as the working atmosphere. But within that, there should be a certain amount of choice. In my subject, choice involves expressing yourself in different media – writing, a tape-recording, a reading, making a selection of poems or perhaps a poster. When I've done tape-recorder work, I've been surprised what some children can do. Children who can't write well can be very good orally.

Andy, the head of chemistry profiled in Chapter 7, sees choice as a means of giving children a sense of ownership of their work, which he finds increases their involvement in it.

Building confidence

Just about all the staff said they thought that building children's confidence was crucial to the development of children's creativity. There can also be a self-fulfilling prophecy effect according to a social work lecturer: 'If you tell people they are creative, they are more likely to be creative'.

A further education art and design lecturer offers some useful insights:

> There seem to be an awful lot of students doing art and design who for one reason or another . . . have problems at home. Confidence has an awful lot to do with it. So we do encourage students to talk to us, because their worries affect their work.
>
> We do seem to have a lot of kids with problems. Art is often seen as a means of keeping difficult kids quiet. Because of that, it's devalued. We get kids who are casualties of that approach coming through to college and doing well. There are a lot of kids with social problems, anorexia, feeling people don't understand them. One of the things we do is to try and put that right, because we've had bad experiences ourselves – not being understood; people thinking you're thick because you can't do maths . . . . In my experience, creative kids either react to bad experiences with a cold shoulder – not caring about others – or by getting very introspective, depressed and down. I had one kid who would just sit under the table, when it all got too much.
>
> They dress differently, our kids. It's not just to do with consciously being different. It's just how they are. They express themselves differently. I think a lot of them rebel against not being encouraged to be creative.
>
> Art is often treated as a recreation for kids who can't do anything else 'Go off and do art'. It isn't actively encouraged. You're lucky if you get a school with an art department that's appreciated. There are some schools like that. You can tell which students have come from a good art department. Some come unable to use even a ruler properly. But the skills we prefer them to have are communication and assertiveness skills, because we know we can build from there. We can teach the practical skills.
>
> In school, personal and social education isn't concentrated on enough for pupils to feel good about themselves. You get a lot of kids who just cannot talk. I don't think they have been encouraged to have any self-esteem. It started when teachers preferred pupils to keep quiet. And usually the disruptive ones are the ones who've had a bad experience and will take someone on, rather than be put down first.
>
> Some students do wonderful work, but they can't even take you complimenting them in the classroom. Not being able to accept that someone feels good about what they've done is an awful thing for young

people. Students need to feel they are worth something. There should be somewhere – and school has to be the place – where they're encouraged to be themselves. If they go home and it's awful, at least there's someone who'll listen to them.

They've got to feel they can trust you. If everyone they've ever encountered has made them feel worthless or useless, at least they can say their teachers value them.

We take them on a one week residential. It's a way of them getting to know us, each other and a different way of teaching. What we try to do is to give them loads and loads of different skills to use. We find it very hard to get through to them at least for the first half term, because they think of every subject as separate – and not part of design as a whole.

They won't talk with us. They're not happy saying how they really think. You can tell when they come round and realize how important it is to them to be doing something creative. When they actually get excited and can talk without being self-conscious, that's when you realize you're beginning to help them and they realize it's important to them. That's what you have to encourage.

After the first year we encourage them to specialize, so they are much more in control of what they do. They set their own projects. They're not led. I think it takes them a year to get away from the idea they had in school – that they're just doing it for the teacher.

A lot of our students have been told they were no-hopers at school, and they come here and then go on to do a degree.

Developing creativity by not doing

Five teachers noted how non-interference helps. Here are some examples of what they had to say:

We can develop creativity by not doing. I mean you need to provide a lot of stimuli, but by not preventing [them] . . . . We're going to try with our nursery children what happens in high school, where children plan what they do and get out their own equipment. The usual thing is for everything to be there for nursery children, so they never have to plan. This spoon-fed approach leads children always to accept things and never to develop themselves.

We don't listen enough. We don't look enough. We're so ham-strung by our own expectations and parents' expectations and outside pressures. It's only when you can stand outside and actually look at what a child is doing, that you realize [the creativity is] there. Children can be encouraged to be creative by less interference. I don't mean less provision or less planning, nor necessarily less structure.

If you're trying to develop creativity in young children, you set up a lot of things and you hope they will interact with them. You talk about what they're doing and show interest, but you don't do everything for them. There always has to be an opening left for them. There's nothing wrong with that, nor with them not always being interested.

Valuing pupils' ideas and contributions

The head of science at a London comprehensive school describes his approach:

I develop creativity by valuing pupils' ideas. I begin by discussing and listening to them. It's important to accept their ideas positively and take them on board, including plausible ideas which have been thought through, but which are not currently accepted. You don't say 'That's stupid'. A lot of science teaching is just accepted theory, but ideas do change. There are other theories. Fashions change about what is accepted and what isn't.

This teacher went on to describe how his school is working towards an independent approach to learning, which is a complete change of style. He is aware that such an innovation has to be a departmental decision and implemented fairly slowly so that staff feel happy about teaching this way:

If you go in and do something revolutionary it could be a flop, because everything is so tight around the school. We're getting there, but we're not there yet. To give pupils complete freedom in one area and restrict them in another could be beneficial, but they might view that freedom in the wrong way – that you're not expecting much of them, when in fact you are expecting more.

Keeping a balanced perspective is important too, according to a junior teacher:

All children should be treated as individuals and should be taught to live their lives in harmony with their fellow human beings. But they must be aware that they are not the centre of the universe. The world should be a better place for the very fact that they are a part of it.

A maths specialist emphasized the importance of respecting a child's need to work independently outside the group. Torrance and Myers (1970) suggest that creativity is encouraged by allowing children to work alone. Shallcross (1985) agrees that they should be allowed some personal space until such time as they are ready to share their ideas with others.

Highly creative children need to have their skills valued by being given challenging work to do:

I have found in twenty years of teaching that the most creative children demand to be given the stimulus to enable them to create or they will either regress into boredom or create mayhem and insist upon using any available work to show their creativity – as I did when I was a child. Creatively gifted children are unhappy if not given the right opportunities, but most children will respond to a creative stimulus, especially in creative writing or drama. Creatively gifted children are often the ones who produce unique pieces of work e.g. a poem early on which is a true poem. I have found this ability comes from within the child and is seldom taught, though it can be encouraged.

(English, art and textiles teacher)

Teachers sharing ideas

Without doubt it is valuable for teachers to get together to discuss what creative ideas they can generate to improve their pupils' learning performance. Here, a Merseyside primary school head describes a change brought about by staff sharing their ideas about teaching reading:

We've changed our approach to reading. This now involves the teacher sharing a book with the children, reading from it, then allowing it to be made available to the children. It's really motivating that the children can read from the teacher's book. It's so simple, yet we missed it for so long. The teacher's book is normally a lovely book on the top shelf that you never see, except at story time, then it goes back on the top shelf.

The effect of teachers' own behaviour

The kinds of teacher behaviour thought to be supportive of creativity were discussed in Chapter 7 – behaviour such as being enthusiastic, confident, willing to take risks. As a deputy head of juniors pointed out 'It is the confident teacher who allows children to be confident within the task. Adults can inhibit creativity by defining the horizon or setting limits. Children learn what is difficult from adults' own limitations or self-image, so adults must not impose their own limitations'.

An office practice lecturer recognized that one's personal enthusiasm could be infectious, but she thought that without teachers acting as catalysts, students would do 'as little as possible, unless motivated to do otherwise'. This is reminiscent of McGregor's Theory X view of human behaviour (McGregor, 1960).

A social care lecturer said he thought that education was about taking risks:

Sometimes things will fall apart, but if you're not prepared to take risks which might result in failure, then you won't get the kind of results the group is capable of. A lot of the time I believe in going out and trying – to see what happens.

I occasionally fall on my face but I think humility is an important characteristic in creative teaching. You say you're sorry and get on with the job. If you're concerned about looking good and close it down, that's a shame. If you can continue with an uncomfortable, difficult situation, some good can come out of it.

THREE TEACHERS' ACCOUNTS OF TEACHING FOR CREATIVITY

A male head of art and design, working in the West Country

You can't teach in terms of what has the seal of approval of the Department for Education. Teaching has to be like personal relationships – you can't insist on attitudes. You can be nice to people and hope they will respond to you. The teaching situation has to be of that order. People being persuaded it's possible, rather than directed – I think this applies to creative work. I think it's very rarely effected by pressure.

I think strategies for getting people to do what you want them to do are very important. So are the conditions that you set up to encourage them to go on . . . to something a bit better next time. This is fundamental. It's not something once in a while; it builds lesson by lesson.

I think there's a danger that because we remember something that the kids did last lesson, we think we can just pick it up again from where we've left off. Whereas they've been in dozens of other lessons with lots of other teachers. So they're probably going to need a bit of time to settle down and think their way into what needs to be done. If there are some who are reluctant to settle down, then you may have to start leading them fairly firmly. But if you start dragooning from the beginning, then you're taking the possibility of self-motivation away from them. Sometimes it's hard to be patient. Five minutes at the beginning of a lesson can seem an awful long time, but it's worth it. If it's something new, then you may have a more formal start. Mostly I start by teaching something – introducing knowledge or skill. Then I give them the opportunity to use it in a personal way. Sometimes this will be more directed and sometimes it will be totally open.

For teachers, the big buzz is starting it with the demonstrations – showing the slides, working up their enthusiasm. Once that's operating and they're all working, I have to find odd jobs to keep me occupied, because they don't need me then. I'm always keen to get on to the next project I'm getting enthusiastic about. I haven't lost interest in the last, but my contribution is mainly over.

A female further education lecturer, working in Shropshire

When I was first brought into FE, there were these young people who were very disillusioned with the school system. To start with, they saw college as another learning experience they didn't want. They wanted to be in work, but couldn't get any.

In the first year we didn't have vocationally-based qualifications and I found the flexibility of being able to devise my own subject area without syllabus constraints great.

I like active teaching. I don't believe in passive learning. Student-centred learning supports creativity. It's not a free for all. You think it through carefully and provide the resources – not necessarily all the resources. You can set something up they've got to deal with – that's promoting creativity, enabling people to learn and sort things out for themselves without restrictions being imposed.

The course objectives were very subject-oriented, so we looked at these and picked out the ones which went together with a view to adopting a much more integrated approach to our modular teaching.

In this course, the young people have to develop a scheme or project – something they would like to carry out in the field, such as in working with elderly people. They have to negotiate with an old people's centre, carry out their project and evaluate it. For example, one of the assignments includes holding a special event in the community. The group has to maybe hold a pantomime, a social afternoon for elderly people or a fun afternoon for children. I give them the basic guidelines and enable them to get a support system going amongst themselves and they do the rest.

They think about financing. They do the fund-raising, health and safety, the content of the programme – the script, characters, costume, scenery; and the client group – is it pitched at the right level? is the venue suitable? – refreshments, resources, costings and so on. From nothing comes a great deal of learning and creativity. Some of the ideas they come up with are original and they really work. The self-confidence and the self-esteem they gain from this is great. You can actually see them grow in confidence.

At first they think they can't do it, because people had always told them they couldn't. It might not be brilliant in terms of professional theatre, but in comparison with what they thought they could achieve, it's brilliant. If they lack confidence, we get a little audience for them to try it out on and then they realize people do respond. It's all to do with confidence and self-esteem, enabling people to realize that they can do things.

We've built up a staff team whose main aim is to give them that confidence and show them they can do it. They do grow in self-esteem over the two years. It's incredible! It's not just us, but the work placement as well and their peers.

But I'm sure being given your own space to grow in confidence does help, as does a great deal of praise. I'm not saying that the FE section's got it all right, because I've worked in various areas and I've seen a lot going wrong.

One thing I have noticed is that students coming into college need to learn new skills, because they've been in a more passive role before and maybe not encouraged to question. We have to be very supportive in encouraging them to question and helping them realize that if they get it wrong, it doesn't matter.

They need the skills to go and research. It took a lot of work at first, to help them realize that even if they've not passed English, they can do just as well. Once they can challenge, explore, question, then their self-confidence grows.

A male art and photography teacher, working in the West Country

I teach traditional creative subjects. I put quite a high stress on individual creativity and building up confidence so that pupils can become aware of the world and explore their personal response to it. In photography, you have to teach this in tandem with a lot of technical skills. As with any other tools, you've got to be able to use them well before you can express yourself as you would wish. So I try and draw the two strands together. Once they've mastered the technical skills, they can push their own creative vision forward. To begin with, it has to be quite structured. So the one takes off from the other.

Confidence building is essential, because without that they won't take any risks, make any mistakes. In school, especially with adolescents, that's the biggest problem. They always want to play safe and take the easy option. If they have a particular idea that they want to express in a certain way – if it doesn't come right first time – they get very disillusioned and frustrated. You've got to encourage them.

SUMMARY

Most of the teachers think that creativity can be developed. Whilst they have some excellent ideas about how this might be achieved, their main focus of attention tends to be on the kind of supportive climate in which creativity can happen or on teaching skills. These skills do not however include problem solving skills, except for one teacher who mentions teaching thinking. But the only method she knows of is brainstorming.

All the evidence suggests that creativity development requires highly skilled teaching and those teachers who value this use terms like *negotiated learning* or *directive opportunism* to describe the kind of balanced approach they regard as most appropriate.

The evidence further suggests that neither highly authoritarian nor *laissez-faire* approaches to teaching are appropriate, something with which most teachers agree. Teachers need to actually teach skills and children need to have the opportunity to get actively absorbed in interesting and relevant learning tasks, either on their own or with others. This involves providing quiet working conditions for this to happen, for at least some of the time.

Teaching for creativity involves a complex mix of variables, many of which staff have highlighted and all of which need to be taken into account.

9

Creativity development – what the teachers did not say

The teachers who took part in Project 1000 have provided some valuable insights into what creativity means to them, how this relates to their teaching and what they think helps and hinders the production of creative work. The main purpose of this chapter is to draw attention to some further approaches used in the development of creativity.

A central issue concerns what is actually meant by the term 'developing creativity'. As we have seen, most of the teachers think that creativity can be developed, yet over 70 per cent of them envisage it as a rare gift. The notion of creativity as a gift implies some kind of God-given endowment or inherited ability. This is frequently associated with the view that highly creative people are in some way qualitatively different from other people. However, no evidence for this view has been found. Instead, the indications are that any differences are in terms of degree rather than kind and that these differences relate to levels of knowledge, skill and motivation (Weisberg, 1986; 1993).

Knowledge, skills and motivation are all things which teachers and lecturers can address. Of course, as Weisberg points out, the production of highly creative work is usually the result of years of effort, but there is no reason why young people cannot become more creative.

PROBLEM SOLVING

Problem solving is a lot more pervasive in learning and thinking than we generally realize. We are constantly making decisions and drawing conclusions, often paying scant attention to the fact that we are solving problems.

Since many creativity development programmes focus on problem solving skills, the intention here is to draw attention to some of the ways they go about this, after briefly exploring how novices and experts differ in the way they solve problems. The assumption often made is that it is the experts who are more likely to produce highly creative work, although this may not always be the case.

The evidence, which Weisberg (1993) and others present, suggests that experts are better than novices at recognizing patterns, seeing analogies, and thinking in terms of underlying principles. For example, in DeGroot's much-quoted study of chess masters, it was noticed that their ability to focus on the right moves was based on their ability to remember patterns of moves as opposed to single moves (DeGroot, 1966). This conclusion has been backed up by Chase and Simon (1973). It has generally been found that people can cope with about seven chunks of information at a time when solving problems. A chunk may be defined as 'any familiar unit of information based on previous learning' (Cohen, Eysenck and LeVoi, 1986, p. 62). It appears that chess masters can cope with larger chunks of information than novices.

Weisberg describes how Chi, Feltovich and Glaser (1981) found the same kind of phenomenon in physics. In this case, the novices focused on the surface appearance of problems, whereas the professors examined the problems in terms of underlying principles, before tackling them. Weisberg compares this with a similar study of radiologists by Lesgold *et al.* (1988). Here the experts first identified the type of problem with which they were dealing, then searched for further information which would confirm or reject their hypothesis. Weisberg describes their willingness to flexibly entertain alternative hypotheses to achieve a good match with the evidence before them. The novices, on the other hand, took much longer to establish an initial diagnosis, but once they had decided on it, they were reluctant to change it. Also, they were more inclined to shape the evidence to match their hypothesis, whilst the experts did the reverse. Weisberg concludes that it is deep immersion in a subject area which enables experts to be aware of underlying principles.

All these findings point to the importance of learning experiences in which children get absorbed and which promote real understanding, as described by Entwistle (1987). There is an issue about the number of areas in which children can be expected to become deeply immersed (Ogilvie, 1974). At the same time, it may be that teachers can to some extent short-circuit this process. A well-structured lecture or presentation can often highlight underlying patterns and principles. But if they are to remember these, young people normally have to interact with the material in some meaningful way (Craik and Lockhart, 1972).

In describing how inventors such as Edison came up with new ideas, Weisberg draws attention to the use of analogical thinking in creative production, as when noticing the similarity between the problem in hand and similar ones experienced previously. He suggests that experience with a wide range of problems helps people to draw such analogies, something which he believes is unlikely to happen spontaneously. There are clear implications for teaching and learning and it is also worth considering whether a neglect of the arts is detrimental to children's ability to reason by analogy.

CREATIVITY DEVELOPMENT PROGRAMMES

Synectics

The Synectics programme devised by Gordon (1961) relies heavily on the use of analogies to generate creative solutions. He stresses that Synectics involves people working more intensively, rather than more easily. The word Synectics comes from 'synergy' which Gordon (1961, p. 3) translates from the Greek as 'the joining together of different and apparently irrelevant elements'. In Synectics, this involves deliberately bringing together different kinds of people to work on problems, with the aim of achieving 'fundamental novelty'. By this Gordon means novelty which has wide applicability. He suggests that Synectics groups should be made up of about five to seven people who differ in terms of their specialist areas, skills and interests. And he recommends including, if possible, a technical expert to play either 'encyclopaedia or devil's advocate' (Gordon, 1961, p. 13). This could be the tutor, a member of the local community or perhaps someone from industry.

Clearly there is most scope for this kind of approach in high school or college. Gordon finds it a particularly helpful approach for scientists, since their lack of arts training has made it difficult for them to break away from old ideas and envisage new ones. Where scientists have allowed their imaginations to wander, this has led to some significant technological breakthroughs. Examples include Einstein, Faraday, Edison and Kekule (Gordon, 1961; and others).

Synectics relies heavily on metaphorical thinking as a means of breaking away from old thought patterns. Gordon (1961) sees this as necessary, because the majority of problems are not new. So there is a need to view problems in new ways, making the familiar strange or making the strange familiar. Metaphorical thinking can help participants adopt a new viewpoint which can afford a fresh insight. According to Gordon, it is a particular kind of metaphor which is required – 'generative' as opposed to 'decorative'.

Gordon describes decorative metaphor as 'after-the-fact', since it reflects what is already known by drawing attention to similarities rather than differences. 'Generative' metaphor, on the other hand, is 'before-the-fact'. It involves linking hitherto unconnected things which are largely different but do have something in common. It is more like the simile, as in 'my love is like a red, red rose', where the points of difference between 'my love' and the rose are actually greater than the points of similarity, but there is an essential similarity and it is this which affords the fresh perspective (Gordon, 1961 p. 106–7).

Synectics employs four levels of metaphor or analogy in an attempt to get new perspectives on familiar problems. These are:

- direct analogy (according to Gordon, the most fruitful source is biology);
- personal analogy;
- symbolic analogy;
- fantasy analogy.

Direct analogy

Direct analogy involves thinking about how similar problems would be solved in other fields, with nature being the most popular. For instance Davis describes how a group of retired people concerned about their personal safety generated ideas by exploring how animals and plants defend themselves. The ideas they thought of included 'spray cans of skunk scent . . . a compressed air can that screams when activated . . . travelling only in groups . . . [and] an eel-like electric shocking stick' (Davis, 1983, p. 68). Direct analogy has been extensively used in design technology.

Personal analogy

In personal analogy, you put yourself in the problem's 'shoes', imagining how you would feel. This technique has also been used in design, in engineering for instance. Gordon also cites the example of Faraday who 'looked . . . into the very heart of the electrolyte endeavoring to render the play of its atom visible to his mental eyes' (Tyndall, 1868, pp. 66–7).

Symbolic analogy

This uses 'objective and impersonal images to describe the problem' (Gordon, 1961, p. 44). The example Gordon gives involves designing a jacking mechanism for moving large objects such as houses.

Fantasy analogy

As the term suggests, this involves generating the most outlandish ideas. The problem solving session described by Gordon (1961, pp. 48, 50) was also concerned with an outlandish problem, which was to 'invent a vapor proof closure for space suits'. Out of the fantasy analogy of 'an insect running up and down the closure manipulating the little latches', a workable solution was derived.

Synectics training is taken very seriously by organizations on both sides of the Atlantic.

The Osborn Parnes creative problem solving process and the Shallcross model

One of the best known approaches to developing creative solutions and putting them into practice evolved out of the work of Alex Osborn. Expanded by Sidney Parnes, it has become known as the Osborn Parnes creative problem solving process (CPS). And of special interest to educators is the Shallcross model which has a close affinity with the Osborn Parnes approach. These models each chart an iterative process involving both analytical and productive thinking.

There are many other training programmes which employ all or part of the Osborn Parnes model. Both Parnes and Shallcross have also championed the development of creative performance by other means (for instance Shallcross, 1985; Parnes, 1992a; 1992b). For example, Parnes has worked extensively with visualization techniques.

Explanations of creative thinking in terms of problem solving strategies are not incompatible with 'mental models' explanations of human cognition. They are simply different levels of explanation (see Chapter 4).

The Osborn Parnes creative problem solving process (CPS)

The Osborn Parnes approach involves individuals learning how to use a problem solving strategy which involves focusing attention on different stages of problem solving activity in order to arrive at an optimum solution (for instance Parnes, 1992a; Osborn, 1993). The process follows a logical sequence. As mentioned above, it is an iterative process involving productive and critical strategies at every phase of the process. According to Parnes, its purpose is to stretch our thinking.

Since the time Alex Osborn laid the groundwork for this programme, an enormous amount of training and consultancy work has blossomed. Much of this capitalizes, in one way or another, on the landmark work done by Osborn and Parnes. An outline sketch of their problem solving process is given below, with an indication of how Parnes sees the facilitators' role (Parnes, 1985; see also Chapter 7). This is no substitute for his own account, which offers many practical suggestions.

Parnes (1985, p. 4) describes the deliberate development of creative behaviour as 'an exaggerated push for change'. He sees this as 'stretching people beyond their normal limits in an oscillating process of imagining and judging during all stages of problem solving – in piling up facts, defining viewpoints of the problem, generating ideas, recognizing criteria and finding ways to ensure the successful acceptance and implementation of ideas'.

He has noticed that the effect of such training is that participants become increasingly able to consider many more factors in a given time in making decisions. This is precisely what skilled thinkers do, as discussed above.

Parnes (1985, pp. 15–47) describes his process as involving six stages:

1 Objective-finding

This involves identifying 'challenges', 'opportunities' and 'ambitions'. Parnes deliberately begins with a step back from the problem as perceived to help people think around the problem and avoid coming to a decision too quickly about what needs to be addressed. It is well known that presented problems do not always reflect the real issues.

2 Fact-finding

Parnes describes this as an elaboration of Objective-finding, in which participants identify all the questions that need to be asked, collect data and build up a clearer picture of the whole situation. Sufficient data needs to be collected to enable the participants to move on, but not so much that they get bogged down. This stage can finish with a bringing together of key elements within the data identified.

3 Problem-finding

Essentially this stage involves attacking the problem in such a way as to get a new perspective. This can be achieved either by broadening the problem to reveal the real issue or by breaking it down into a series of sub-problems, each beginning with 'In what ways might I (or we)?', to give the feeling that change is possible.

Parnes provides a series of everyday examples to illustrate this phase. One relates to improving an outdoor grill. Here, breaking down the problem would involve asking questions like 'In what ways might I . . . make the grill easy to clean *or* keep the smoke from getting to us?'.

He suggests that one effective way of broadening the problem is by asking 'Why?'. For example 'Why improve the outdoor grill?' can be widened into 'How to enjoy eating out of doors?'. Parnes has lots of ideas for breaking through to new perspectives when no solution is immediately apparent.

He recommends that, towards the end of this stage, the focus should be narrowed to 'the most intriguing' problem-statement to increase the probability that participants get beyond conventional solutions in the time available. Interestingly, he has found that no matter which problem-statement is selected, this has the effect of stimulating ideas relevant to the whole problem, because the exercise has had the effect of bringing them to the forefront of awareness.

4 Idea-finding

Essentially this involves finding possible solutions. Parnes has lots of excellent and fun suggestions for stimulating ideas, including the use of analogies. He stresses the need for getting participants' thinking to go beyond what he calls 'Level 1' brainstorming, which he regards as merely sharing experiences without fear of being judged and he makes the point that a lot of CPS sessions in which people are inexperienced in this technique never get beyond this level.

But Parnes envisages two further levels which he regards as valuable. The second level is where one has 'run out of things to say' so there is no option but to 'deliberately combine, rearrange or adapt ideas . . . in new ways'. The third level he describes as effortless, as when writing takes over from the writer.

5 Solution-finding

The label for this stage can be a source of confusion, since the search here is for criteria rather than solutions. The suggested method of identifying suitable criteria for evaluating the ideas generated involves both productive and critical thinking.

Parnes makes the important point that 'the application of criteria is always implicit . . . at the end of every step of the process . . . . The difference is that it becomes "explicit" in Solution-finding'.

6 Acceptance-finding

Once the ideas have been evaluated according to the criteria selected, all that is required is to think of how to get the ideas into operation. Needless to say Parnes sees this stage as involving both productive and critical thinking too.

This problem solving process may seem quite laborious but with practice it can be quite a speedy one and very productive. Parnes sees this process as continuous. Nothing is final. Everything is relative. Today's best plan becomes tomorrow's challenge for improvement.

Parnes (1985, p. 47) comments:

> If you are gaining a more creative attitude, you are probably 'knowing' CPS better than you would by gaining the fullest intellectual understanding of the specifics of the CPS model. The more creative attitude can become a way of life rather than a set of procedures. With it you can invent your own CPS model and techniques.

He stresses that the purpose of the model is to help people develop such an attitude and he provides further examples of how such an attitude might affect one's approach.

Parnes stresses how important it is that the facilitator helps participants develop their own problem solving skills, rather than imposing his or her own opinions on them. But this does not involve a *laissez-faire* approach. On the contrary, the facilitator's role is quite demanding. Parnes's (1985) guidelines for facilitators are highly recommended.

The Shallcross approach

When she was a schoolteacher, Dorie Shallcross's innovative approach to teaching and learning attracted the attention of Alex Osborn, who invited her to join him in his work. Her achievements since then have been most impressive, including a double presidency of the Creative Education Foundation. She first introduced creativity development into her classroom by getting her school's headteacher to agree that, providing she covered the required curriculum in four days, she could teach in her preferred way on the fifth.

Shallcross employs somewhat different terminology from Parnes, although the process she charts is similar. Her approach to developing creative thinking is easy to use in the classroom.

Shallcross (1985, p. 96) distinguishes between 'primary creativity', which she sees as a natural problem solving process which can operate without conscious awareness, and 'secondary creativity', a deliberate thinking process like the one outlined below.

Shallcross (1985, pp. 97–105) suggests five stages, adding practical suggestions for how these might be dealt with in the classroom.

1 Orientation

Here the aim is to establish why one wants to solve a problem or aim for a goal. The idea is to envisage the problem in greater depth, so that you have 'more to work with, suggesting [clues towards] a more workable solution' and she has some useful suggestions for how this might be achieved in the classroom.

2 Preparation

This stage is concerned with factual data rather than feelings. Its purpose is to identify what you know and what you need to know. Shallcross maintains that people don't always give themselves enough credit for what they already know. She suggests looking at every aspect of the problem, listing what is already known and what needs to be found out, together with a list of possible sources, including unusual ones.

3 Ideation

The purpose of this stage is to generate solution ideas. Shallcross recommends spending ten minutes on solo brainstorming (she regards pacing as quite important), 'trying hard to apply the ground rules: defer judgement, freewheel, strive for quantity, hitchhike on previous ideas'. She is not concerned if people generate conventional ideas, since they could be usefully combined with something else later on, but she does want people to really stretch their thinking. When the time is up, she suggests a change of activity before spending a further ten minutes on brainstorming, using one's previous list to hitchhike or make new associations and aiming to double one's output. This can be done alone or in a group.

Shallcross offers useful guidelines on managing a session and proposes a combination of individual and group brainstorming.

4 Evaluation

Here Shallcross warns us to beware of rejecting ideas which have real potential. However, she recommends an initial intuitive screening (if a lot of ideas have been generated) to get down to about twenty-five. At the same time the idea is not to reject other ideas completely in case they are useful later on. Importantly, she counsels against being over cautious, suggesting that one or two 'far-outs' be retained 'for balance'.

Shallcross regards the selection of criteria as crucially important. About five or six are recommended, with weighting being given to the important ones and she offers guidelines for their use.

5 Implementation

This involves a series of questions we need to consider, such as; What needs to happen first? Will anyone else be involved? Who do I need to persuade about my ideas? – and so on.

Apart from devising this model (which has only been briefly outlined here) and suggesting how it might be implemented in the classroom, Shallcross has many other suggestions for related curriculum activities. These work well with both children and adults.

Building on Land's work (Land, 1973), Shallcross (1985, pp. 24–8) describes four stages which reflect progress as one becomes increasingly creative. She illustrates her argument with an analogy. The analogy she uses – learning to play the piano – also serves to illustrate how applicable this description is to any skill. The stages and the analogy are combined and summarized below.

1 Formative stage

This involves getting to grips with a new environment and feeling secure in it. For the beginning pianist this would involve 'learning the keyboard, learning the notes, co-ordinating your fingers, gaining control'.

2 Normative stage

Now the aim is to be one of the gang, not thought of as different. Peers exert influence and one may feel self-conscious about any differences. In learning the piano, this involves 'trying to make the music sound like music you've heard before, hoping people will recognize the songs and pieces you play, copying the style of playing of a pianist you admire'.

3 Integrative stage

The individual no longer finds it appealing to be just like everyone else. The sameness 'becomes boring and no longer useful. One begins to appreciate what is different within oneself and the differentness of others'. There is a 'desire to share differentness, thereby enriching one's own environment and contributing to the enrichment of others' environments'. The individual develops a sense of pride in his or her uniqueness and greater confidence in 'a more finely defined self.'

In learning the piano, this involves 'gaining enough confidence to integrate a style of your own with the printed music, trying to interpret the composer, sensing a mutuality with the composer and his or her music'.

4 Transformational stage

At this point, one realizes that to grow, one must move on. Sharing of oneself with others no longer seems to offer any opportunities for improvement. The individual feels the need for a major change in 'life and/or lifestyle . . . a crisis time [of] letting go of what has been pleasing and secure'. At this point, the individual either forges ahead or regresses. Forging ahead signifies 'the beginning of another cycle and new struggles for identity and personal space, literally a transformation'. Regressing may be more comfortable but is unlikely to lead to a breakthrough.

In the piano example, this entails 'composing your own music, rearranging existing music, taking up another instrument, beginning a new cycle of growth'.

Both Parnes and Shallcross recognize the need for the development of all kinds of skills which support creative outcomes and are actively involved in exploring these.

In the models outlined above, the term 'problem solving' is employed in the everyday sense of coping with problems where there is no obvious solution. This is usual in the literature on creativity. However, as mentioned earlier, we are constantly engaged in problem solving

Other tools and techniques

A whole range of tools and techniques may be employed as an aid to producing creative outcomes and these may be incorporated into creative problem solving programmes. One is attribute listing (Crawford, 1978) which is widely used in devising new products or thinking of ways to improve a situation. This technique has two main variants, 'attribute modifying' and 'attribute transferring' (Davis, 1983). The former involves simply identifying all the attributes of an object or variables in a situation, holding one constant, then altering each of the other attributes or variables in different ways and assessing the effects, as in the scientific method.

Checklists of verbs have been devised as reminders of all the different ways in which variables may be altered (for instance Osborn, 1993; Davis, 1983). Pupils can have an instructive and fun lesson, systematically altering attributes of products or situations to find out 'What would happen if?'.

Attribute transferring involves the transfer of attributes from one situation to another, as in Synectics and the informal analogical thinking used by inventors. Other techniques (together with additional variants on attribute listing) are included in VanGundy (1984; 1988; 1992).

THE USE OF CREATIVE PROBLEM SOLVING PROGRAMMES

The creative problem solving strategies and techniques described above are geared to cope with unclear situations and difficult problems. Even when solutions seem obvious, we cannot always be sure that we have selected the right ones. Practice in searching for alternative perspectives and solutions may well lead us to be more questioning of 'obvious' conclusions.

There are numerous training programmes on offer, many of which owe their origins to the landmark work highlighted in this chapter. Parnes (1992a) offers evidence for the effectiveness of these kinds of programmes. Both the Osborn Parnes and Shallcross approaches allow participants to address self-selected problems and issues. This applied approach makes learning relevant and meaningful and may assist participants in seeing the relevance of these transferable skills. It is quite possible to combine techniques and approaches. Stein (1994b; 1994c) provides an excellent review of a wide range of strategies for stimulating thinking.

We still need to know why these kinds of programmes work. Various explanations have been put forward, based on a whole range of psychological perspectives. Since there is no evidence to suggest that any unusual thinking processes are involved, the most plausible explanation would seem to be that they serve as *attention-directing device*s – helping participants to

• focus on the various aspects of problems or situations;
• learn how to use various tactics to interact generatively and/or analytically with the problem content;
• increase their motivation in pursuit of their goals.

Few educational systems require (or indeed allow) young people to engage in these kinds of applied learning activities, although the British National Curriculum now requires pupils to engage in problem solving more than it did previously (Perkin, 1995). If we agree with Perkins (1981, p. 274) and regard creativity as 'the mind's best work', then it follows that the whole curriculum needs to be delivered in a way which addresses every aspect of creativity development. If and when this is achieved, developing creativity and providing good education may be regarded as synonymous.

SUMMARY

This chapter has outlined some of the landmark educational programmes which have enabled individuals and organizations all over the world to produce creative work – something which many educational systems neglect. Evidence for the effectiveness of these programmes is available in the literature. The work described in this chapter has spawned a great deal of educational material and development programmes, the quality of which is likely to be variable. It is quite possible to explain, in psychological terms, the function which such programmes serve, without resorting to explanations couched in terms of peculiar or mysterious processes.

10

Overcoming difficulties

Never accept that [a problem] can't be solved; understand that in order to solve it you're going to have to break down some structural barriers; and don't *ever* think that the solution is going to be easy.

(Shirley Brice Heath, in Shekerjian, 1991, p. 134, original emphasis)

The purpose of this chapter is to highlight the kinds of hindrances teachers find make their teaching less effective than it might be. Most of the factors cited are beyond teachers' immediate control (see Table 10.1). Many of the problems are about the resourcing of education, but some staff also identify their personal insecurities as inhibiting.

These obstacles cause them a lot of stress. A Northern Ireland primary teacher sums up the feelings of many staff:

Frankly, morale is very low. They are killing the enjoyment we had. I really think we are being tortured. The pressure is unbelievable and the criticism unfair. I think we are a very dedicated bunch by and large. I think teachers love their work. It's a vocation. People who don't know the first thing about teaching are dictating to us and they're killing all that great enthusiasm and joy. I think it's a tragedy. It's as sad as that. It's people who don't know what it's like to be in a teaching situation who are dictating. I think we should have more say as people who know best. I think sometimes you should go to the people who are on the ground – even if just to consult them. I think a good teacher can keep the creativity bit, even in maths – the investigative aspect. But you have to work hard at it. It's an uphill struggle.

Another West Belfast primary teacher had this to say: 'I'm lucky that there is a friendly openness among the staff I work with. You can talk about a problem and there's a great exchange of ideas, which is a great help when you're in the classroom developing creativity'.

The difficulties the teachers faced did not appear to diminish their motivation to give of their best for their pupils. This sentiment is backed up by Broadfoot *et al.* (1993, p. 127) who compared teaching situations in French and English primary schools:

Why do English primary teachers continue to struggle with the impossible task they set themselves? Certainly not for any extrinsic reward or for public

Table 10.1   The main factors which teachers find counter-productive (N= 1028)

Constraint	% of teachers finding this a constraint
Inadequate resources	52
Inadequate preparation time	48
Over-large classes	44
Excessive non-teaching workload	34
Excessive teaching load	32
Unsuitable accommodation	30

Source: Adapted from Fryer, 1989.

approbation or ease of execution. Perhaps it has something to do with their experience of working with children, and of responding to their individual needs; from witnessing children's pleasure in their own creativity, which was the core of professional motivation of the primary teachers in this study'.

PERSONAL INSECURITIES

The greatest mistake you can make in life is to be continually fearing you will make one.

(Elbert Hubbard, *The Note Book*, 1927)

Teachers are all too aware of how inhibiting their own insecurities can be:

When we get it wrong is when we get too bogged down in the institution of school. We create rules to make life easier, but sometimes this makes things more difficult and we restrict the kids. Sometimes our egos get too big and we become frightened of kids becoming too clever. It's quite threatening to say I don't know. You have to let go of something to be able to do that.

(art teacher, female)

Set procedures can save a lot of time and can contribute to the smooth running of a school or college, but as this teacher recognizes, excessive bureaucracy can be really counter-productive. According to Storr (1988), undue reliance on bureaucratic rules and procedures may be symptomatic of personal insecurity. Storr suggests that people who lack a sense of security in other aspects of their lives may find reassurance in institutional rules and procedures. Whatever the reasons, it certainly seems worthwhile examining the opportunity cost of bureaucracy.

Feeling unsure about one's personal skills may be counter-productive to teaching for creativity. For example, a junior teacher described how her lack of self-confidence about drama teaching prevented her from using educational drama as much as she would have liked. Educational drama can be invaluable in developing creativity. It allows children to exercise imaginative skills, helping them see things from different points of view, building their confidence and improving their communication skills.

This teacher felt particularly uncomfortable about doing drama with classes she did not know well. It was less of a problem with her own class, because she knew exactly how much freedom to allow them and they understood the limits of her tolerance. Her lack of confidence was not entirely counter-productive, however. It did help her to understand just how threatened the really anxious children in her class felt about doing drama. To make them feel more secure, she used subdued lighting. This worked well.

Sometimes one's own feelings of insecurity are attributed to others. One teacher whose overall responses reflect either a very dry sense of humour or an extreme need to be in control identifies 'insufficient pupils of the right type' as the main reason for not teaching in his preferred way. This sounds like reports of the wrong kind of snow bringing rail services to a halt!

Shallcross (1985, p. 67) lists a comprehensive set of psychological factors which inhibit teachers. These include 'habit, the assumed expectations of others, failure to be aware of all the available information, lack of effort and assumed or self-imposed boundaries or limitations'.

Activity 6

What self-imposed barriers do you create? What other barriers stop you from achieving your goals? How real are they? Is there a way round them?

Encouragingly, Torrance and Myers (1970) have found that teachers who are positive about creativity can make all kinds of mistakes, yet their students carry on learning and growing creatively.

SOCIAL CONSTRAINTS

Inadequate communication between schools

Teachers who took part in the Project 1000 exploratory interviews felt impeded by the lack of communication amongst schools at different levels in a tier. They felt that there was scope for improvement. Some staff did not know enough about the aims of the schools to which their pupils would progress. For example, a middle school science teacher said she hoped she was preparing her pupils well for high school by encouraging them to think for themselves and work independently. At the same time she was afraid she was doing them a disservice, making adjustment to high school difficult, especially if the high school were fairly formal. However, she justified her approach by saying that pupils would ultimately 'have to think for themselves' – even if they did not have to do this in high school!

Another middle school teacher said how disappointed she was to find that her hard work in encouraging children to participate in class discussion is not continued in high school. So often children who come back to visit her describe how they have been discouraged from contributing to high school discussions, because they have 'already had their turn'.

A high school English teacher also bemoaned the lack of communication among schools, 'Some teachers seem to assume that if children have not acquired certain skills when they leave one school, they will acquire them higher up the system. Schools higher up tend to think such skills should have been acquired lower down'. A high school textiles teacher remarked how often she comes across children who have reached high school 'without knowing how to hold scissors or lacking the confidence to draw something'. She thinks this derives from a shortage of staff lower down the system. At the same time, she is quick to praise feeder schools for the wonderful job they do on the whole.

Parents

A number of staff feel threatened by the attitudes of some of the parents they encounter. They feel under pressure to 'teach to please the parents' even when this conflicts with children's educational needs. This appears to be a particularly acute problem in predominantly middle class areas. Middle class parents are perceived as being most anxious for their children to do well. An infant teacher who felt threatened in this way said that parents do not always appreciate her strategies. When she encourages her pupils to work creatively, she is accused of 'just playing'. The children in question are five- to six-year-olds.

Here is just one example of the unfortunate consequences of misplaced parental pressure. It concerns a craft lesson. The teacher was so concerned that the children should achieve good results for parents that she had gone to a great deal of trouble to produce templates for some simple models she wanted her class to make. In many instances she did the work for them. The children merely acted as assistants, holding scissors or glue sticks for the teacher. Needless to say, all the finished models looked exactly alike!

In contrast, another infant teacher who happened to be working in an inner-city school showed her pupils just how much their individual art was valued. Every picture produced was entirely the child's own work. All were then carefully mounted for display. The achievements of these infants 'stole the show' in the 'Creativity in schools' exhibition described in Chapter 1.

Another teacher described how she felt that 'there's a conflict within me. On the one hand there are the new teaching methods where children don't sit in regimented rows . . . on the other hand, there's parental pressure'.

Indeed, quite a few primary staff feel obliged to have the children produce rows and rows of sums to please parents, despite believing that a different approach is required. A London primary teacher explains that:

The kind of thing parents expect doesn't necessarily match our objectives. For instance in maths, parents are interested in just a page of sums – so you've got this pressure. In language and reading, they're looking at a certain age and comparisons with the best. I understand this. I've got three children myself. As a teacher I think you've got to take parents wishes into account, so I'm paying attention to things that aren't my priorities.

The children are pressured too, if parents feel they are not doing well. You don't want them to feel inadequate, so I sometimes spend more time than I should on areas I wouldn't choose to from an educational point of view, because I want a good relationship with the parents. I want parents to be happy. They're not so relaxed as ten to fifteen years ago. They have worries that standards have fallen. That isn't my experience. It doesn't seem any worse, but parents are worried – because of the bad press, I think.

A maths specialist working in the North of England makes the same point:

There's still an attitude, especially at this school, that [parents] expect to see rows and rows of sums. We have a lot of maths games. They're getting first-hand experience, but not writing in their books, so there's not a lot to show for it. We've done a lot of investigative work, but not a lot in books.

However the parents linked with this teacher's school are being successfully 'educated' about new developments in maths.

Accountability to parents is now a key part of the official educational agenda in Britain. Good working relationships with parents are clearly advantageous to staff and pupils alike. On the whole, schools value the real contribution parents and other members of the local community can make to the children's education and the life of the school.

A particularly far-sighted deputy head had very successfully engaged parents' collaboration in their children's education long before accountability to parents became formalized. He began by running a series of informative sessions for parents, explaining why the teachers were teaching in the way they did. This helped parents and teachers alike. The result has been a cohesive and enlightened group working together for the children's benefit. Sadly, many teachers have found that the parents they most want to meet never come near the school.

Colleagues

A Belfast junior teacher described how

you feel obliged to please other parties in the school, which means that you can't feel happy going ahead with something if it's not leading to a display on the wall. I'm not specially good at art and craft and mounting things and making them look pretty. It does take time. One day I shocked myself, saying to the children 'We have to do this for the wall'. I thought 'Am I doing this for the wall?' That made me think.

For a drama teacher the most counter-productive feature of her working environment is her colleagues' lack of understanding of the needs of her subject:

> The length of single lessons is only 35 minutes. Some schools do allow doubles, but my experience with drama teaching is that we have 35 minutes, which in reality is often reduced to 20 minutes. They will argue against drama or music and will always win in a battle over time allocation. There's a lack of understanding generally from senior colleagues who have the responsibility for implementing the timetable. Other subjects take priority.

For a lecturer working with students with learning difficulties, the most constraining factor is 'people seeing things in subject areas – in little boxes, instead of seeing that things can be integrated and that you're not just "in a classroom". You might want to access lots of other things – computers, art and crafts and so on'.

RESOURCING OF EDUCATION

Many British teachers are operating under difficult, in some cases appalling, conditions. The main problems relate to inadequate teaching resources, lack of time and having to teach large groups.

Inadequate teaching resources

Lack of resources is the teachers' most common complaint. The shortages identified include maths and scientific equipment, up-to-date textbooks and design materials. One textiles tutor actually had to build her own design table, because her college had insufficient funds to buy one:

> There's never enough money to do what I want. I like to introduce something new to the students every year. I wanted a textiles printing table. They're really expensive! There was no money so I built one with the help of another tutor for a third of the price. We felt quite proud of ourselves, but now people expect us to do more and more.

Although lack of money or lack of resources is the stated difficulty, the real issue is one of priorities at all levels – school, government and society in general, as argued by Torrance (1967) and Stein (1984). Perhaps the worst case of inadequate resources identified in Project 1000 is a London primary school where even the most basic resources are in short supply:

> It's getting worse. A lot of basic things, even paper, are not readily available, or pens, pencils – basic tools . . . . There is a good 'scrap scheme' where you can get waste materials from industry. The things provided by the authority are more valuable, but we know they're going to run out if we use them too freely.
>
> (primary teacher, female)

Should children really have to rely on 'scrap' for their education?

Time problems

Lack of preparation time was perceived as the next most important problem for the teachers. But lack of time affects many other aspects of their jobs, including advising and counselling pupils, marking work and dealing with problem children.

> I'm woefully inadequate on preparation and keeping up with ideas. I teach thirty-five periods a week; I'm overloaded. It's ridiculous that teachers are expected to do so much. Some classes have more pupils than is safe in one room. I only have thirty-five minutes a week for careers teaching.
>
> (high school teacher, male)

> Since I started teaching in the Sixties, the job's changed. We're doing more social work as well. I think that's right, but I've so many things to do that I don't do any of them well. I work from 8.30 a.m. to around 7.45 p.m. That's not counting parents' evenings. But I know however hard I work, I still can't get it all done. It's like juggling. Sometimes I've got to set a Saturday aside to catch up with marking. It's crisis management all the time.
>
> As a year head, if a child does something bad, you have to deal with it on the spot, but there's no time to stand aside and question teaching practices. There's no time to do the useful work of building relationships, identifying troublesome children, spending time with them to praise, encourage and prevent crises. You know you should be doing it. We know exactly what should be done, but we can't for lack of time.
>
> (high school teacher, female)

This teacher pointed out how much better things could be if teachers were not constantly exhausted and if they had more time to prepare stimulating lessons. She said she didn't think it was fair to the children to teach in a tired state. Nor did she want tired staff teaching her own children.

Over-large classes

This was the third most common complaint. For instance, a head of chemistry said how difficult over-crowding made GCSE assessment: 'The classes are too big – twenty-six in a laboratory designed for twenty. Twenty is the maximum for GCSE practical groups, if we are to assess effectively. We suffer, but it's the children who get the raw deal'.

The same sentiment was echoed by other teachers, for example

> I feel strongly that the large classes are a major factor in restricting the creativity development of individual pupils and it is causing discipline problems in the classroom system. With 5–13-year-olds, fifteen is the optimum number for the effective teaching of each individual, enabling the teacher to devote sufficient time to each pupil and bring out their creative potential.
>
> (middle school teacher)

We had quite low numbers, twenty-five to twenty-six, and that enabled me to be more relaxed. It enabled you to treat children as individuals and not to work in tightly organized groups. Next year, I shall have thirty-two, so you have to be much more tightly organized and group [the children] according to ability, which I haven't done for a long time. This does have advantages, but I feel worried about whether I can keep track of what everyone is doing.

(primary teacher)

Most staff regard a class size of twenty pupils as ideal. They point out how easily they could raise academic standards with this number of children to teach. In a comparison of French and English primary schools, Broadfoot *et al.* (1993) describe how teachers in English primary schools have to typically cope with classes of around thirty, whilst their French counterparts only have about twenty pupils in a class and these are a more homogeneous group.

Excessive administrative load

Just over a third of teachers saw burgeoning bureaucracy as counter-productive. Many described how they had chosen the teaching profession, because they enjoyed teaching. They now feel so bogged down with administrative duties, that they scarcely have time to teach.

Unsuitable accommodation

The most often stated problem about accommodation is its lack of suitability for the kind of teaching taking place. For example, an electronics lecturer complained that his laboratory is housed in totally unsuitable Victorian accommodation. Furthermore, experimental equipment has to be dismantled at the end of every lesson so that other groups can use the room, something he finds really disruptive. This tutor has partly got around this problem by taking his students to work in the National Museum of Photography whenever possible. But this facility is in another city.

Several teachers pointed out how much easier it would be to create an atmosphere conducive to learning in purpose-built accommodation. An art and photography teacher said he would like a good teaching room:

one which is comfortable and different from the others, so that pupils can see immediately the subject you're teaching. If you've just got a general classroom, it's very difficult to create the right atmosphere. But if they come into a room where they know what work is expected and it's all around, then it's a safe environment to be creative.

What he really wants is a multi-equipped studio with lots of different tools and media around. His sentiments are echoed by a Merseyside art and design teacher. As far as ordinary classroom provision is concerned the following comment is fairly typical:

There aren't enough sinks. In my last school there was a sink in every classroom, a carpeted area and bays for different activities. Here the classrooms are depressing. With wooden floorboards, you can't do movement in the classroom; there's only one hall for six classes, so it's restricting. And it makes an awful noise when the children move around, chairs scraping and so forth. [It's] very distracting for the other children. Also we have only one plug in the classroom, so that means wires have to trail across the carpeted area, which isn't good.

Multiple problems

Some of the teachers face a multiplicity of problems, like this primary head:

I've been a head for twelve months. The changes I thought I would be able to make are constantly being constrained by mountains of paper. The building's a problem which takes time to sort out. It's one hundred per cent rotten and it's too small. It takes an inordinate amount of time to sort out and this is not my main role. The school is under-resourced. There's no clay. The toys are worn out. We got one computer twelve months ago. I've spent a lot of time trying to get resources.

There was insufficient help for group activities, but I'm building up parental involvement. You've got to prepare for that, making teachers feel secure. We've got some paired reading going. It takes time. It may take three years to see results. It's not under-resourcing as such, it's just that my priorities are different from my predecessor's. Submitting bids for extra funding takes a lot of time.

The textiles teacher who built her own table provides a further, if less severe example, of how teachers often have to cope with a multiplicity of constraints:

The main constraint I have is the room I have to work in. My subject has both dirty and clean aspects, so the clean design has to be at one end and the dirty dyeing at the other. The classes I teach are too big and they are of mixed ability, with a lot of personal problems, so I have to play lots of different roles. There seem to be an awful lot of students doing art and design who . . . have problems at home. I have to play a counselling role. I wouldn't divorce listening from my teaching, but it cuts down time for other things. I'm stretched all the time, though I do have the help of a part-time textiles specialist, which is great. It's nice to have someone to bounce ideas off too.

But it was the primary school heads who seemed most stressed. They often have to deal with administrative duties and teach at the same time. Quite a lot of them have to double up as supply staff, often at very short notice. The head of a school with 87 pupils on roll describes himself as having two full-time jobs 'teaching 6–7-year-olds all day, every day and running the school, which involves dealing with visitors, prospective parents, builders, gas and electricity representatives, delivery people and the police, who all expect to be attended to during the normal school day'.

THE EFFECTS OF CONSTRAINTS ON TEACHERS

The ambivalence which teachers feel about their working situation is neatly captured in the following extract from Nias (1989), quoted in Broadfoot *et al.* (1993, p. 126):

> The feelings associated with teaching always seem to be contradictory. Successful teachers learn to keep them in balance, but even they swing, sometimes by minutes, between love and rage, elation and despair. To 'be' a teacher is to be relaxed and in control, yet tired and under stress, to feel whole while being pulled apart; to be in love with one's work, but daily to talk of leaving it. It is to learn to live with unresolved uncertainties, contradictions and dilemmas; to accept that the very nature of teaching is paradoxical.

Of course teachers can and have been able to draw on their own considerable resources to overcome the difficulties they face. The question is whether they should have to. The time and energy spent battling against or ingeniously skirting around obstacles detracts from their teaching. A maths teacher, working with children with learning difficulties in a Welsh high school, remarked 'I think the public want a better educational system and would be prepared to pay for it'. He just might be correct.

COPING WITH CONSTRAINTS

Meanwhile, here are just two examples of teachers getting around the constraints they face. The first is a lecturer:

> I teach people with learning difficulties. When we apply for resources, the higher grade courses get priority. I've got around that, because I've been prepared to go out and make things work, but some people don't have the confidence or the courage to do that. But I keep persevering for resources and it's time-consuming.
>
> In my training, I found I was different from the others on the course in a lot of ways. I was 'a pain', if you like, because I would challenge objectives, standards, performances and conditions. I would challenge certain areas – 'How can you do this?', 'Who is to say?'.
>
> [A small group of us] who challenged and thought 'divergently' were made to feel lacking in some way. As the course developed, I realized what they were actually doing was encouraging us to be more conforming to situations.
>
> We had this big debate on creativity with a psychologist. From then, I started to feel good . . . . From that lecture, four or five of us became fully

aware that the way we'd go about teaching was creative – because we'd do things differently. We'd look for all sorts of different ways that we could make learning imaginative and exciting for the students.

(FE Lecturer)

I suspect my tremendous workload is self-inflicted choice, but I really want this to be a good school and I think if I work hard that will have an effect. There were all sorts of problems with the school when I came here. It was under threat of closure and it's gone from that to being one of the most over-subscribed schools in the area, in four years. I don't think that can happen unless a lot of people work themselves into the ground to do it.

I knew when I took the job that that's what it was going to be like – that it wouldn't happen slowly. In another situation it might need to happen more slowly. I think the situation here required it and that's why I've got this workload.

Before I came here it was very under-subscribed and local parents were putting their children on trains and buses to get them away. It had a reputation for being extremely violent. I don't think it was as violent as its reputation, but there were a lot of fights both within the school and in its vicinity. No local inhabitant would go to the shops at lunch-time because they were frightened of the children, particularly the bigger ones. It was fairly normal for the kids to swear at staff and staff felt fairly powerless to do much about it. On the whole the school just lacked direction. There was a long period with no head. That was no-one's fault – four years with no head. I think the morale of the teaching staff just sank. That got conveyed to the children. There was a lack of purpose about the school and discipline just broke down.

[*Interviewer*: How did you manage to turn it round?] Well, I think when you're new there are certain expectations and hopes that you will do something about it and people want to give you a chance. I tried to set out very clearly for staff and pupils what the parameters were and what my philosophy was. I had a staff meeting on the first morning and I read out a twenty-four page speech to them. I said 'I will never do that again because it's not my style'. My style is actually quite informal, but I just wanted to let them know what I'd brought with me. I didn't think we had time for them to spend years finding out what I was about.

I tried to come in with very high expectations of the children. For example, the school was about to be re-decorated and a dark green colour had been chosen so that the graffiti wouldn't show. So I got the school painted white and told the children it was on the assumption that they weren't going to write anything on it.

I tried to raise their morale with a lot of emphasis on how the school would be a great school and how they were great kids. They listened because they knew everyone thought the school was awful and they were awful. I did kick a few out – about six in my first year, which is quite a lot. Now expulsions are very rare.

I talked about behaviour. They weren't going to swear at staff and they weren't going to fight. I shut my door in the first year and walked around everywhere in and out of the school, so they knew that if they were transgressing, they would be caught. But on the whole, staff and pupils were quite pleased that someone was coming along saying 'This is not acceptable and this is why'. In fact, discipline was the easiest thing to sort out. It was as if everyone were waiting for someone to come along and say that. Since then the discipline has gone from strength to strength.

The staff are great! We know who the enemy is – and it isn't each other. We've kept that uppermost in our minds. I need to be working with staff. I couldn't cope with continual confrontation all the time. We've got involved in a lot of new developments and initiatives and it's helped to take the school forward.

(headteacher, Inner London high school)

Shekerjian (1991, p. 25) describes how focusing on 'something perceived as distinctly larger than their own tiny vulnerable beings' gave the MacArthur winners she interviewed the courage to take risks. The MacArthur awards are American awards for personal achievement in any field.

Here is how award-winning teacher, Debbie Meier, describes herself to Shekerjian:

I'm willing to take on risk because I'm invested in the project and because I believe in what we are doing here and want it to succeed. The drive is towards that, towards the goal, not the problems. Of course, I don't like to fail. I don't like to make mistakes. I'm afraid of looking foolish. I'm afraid of dying. But I'm not afraid of risk, because risk is part of change, and change is what new ideas are all about.

(Shekerjian, 1991, p. 24)

Clearly Meier's goals gave her confidence. The importance of self-confidence and the willingness to take risks are recurrent themes in the literature on creative people (see Chapter 3). Shekerjian recounts how persistence and determination help another MacArthur award winning teacher, Shirley Brice Heath, to succeed in her objectives

If there is a key to my progression, I think it is the fact that I never accepted any sort of constraint but immediately moved out beyond it. For me 'can't' simply isn't acceptable and I urge my students to get it out of their vocabulary. I want them to kick against any boundaries that are set up and to figure out how they can shift resources to move beyond them. It takes imagination and hard work, because, as far as I'm concerned, there have been no good solutions to problems that haven't demanded a lot of hard work.

(Shekerjian, 1991, p. 132)

SUMMARY

The most common constraint perceived by teachers was a lack of resources, which in some instances was a very severe problem. Almost as common was a feeling that they had insufficient time to prepare lessons and attend to other parts of their jobs. Large class sizes added to their difficulties, something which appears to be getting worse.

Quite a lot of staff described how they had chosen teaching, because they liked working with children, but they increasingly felt that expanding bureaucracy was taking them away from the work they were most skilled to do. Primary head teachers in particular found it stressful trying to juggle teaching and administrative demands.

Other people's expectations or perceived expectations had made some teachers feel quite inhibited. Inappropriate parental expectations caused problems for certain staff, especially where parents were excessively anxious for their children to do well. What was remarkable was the extraordinary resourcefulness of staff in the face of profound difficulties and in some cases a multiplicity of constraints. How much better they could do their jobs if education were valued enough for them to work at their optimum capacity!

ALTERNATIVE JOBS

When teachers were asked what their ideal job would be, some said this was the job they already had; some wanted a promotion; some wanted to stay in education, but in a different capacity. Quite a few wanted to pursue their specialist subject rather than teach it. But here is what the rest said they would like to be:

• sports commentator • entertainments manager • working on a liner •
museum curator • veterinary nurse • veterinary surgeon • landscape gardener

• professional footballer • national park warden • professional golfer • doctor • meteorologist • actress • Blue Peter presenter • cook • chef • licensee • orchestral manager • musical director • diplomat • dog breeder • dentist • bus conductor • dressmaker • novelist • number 3 batsman for England • Minister of Education • farmer • farmer's wife • wealthy wife • society hostess • coffee shop manager • financial advisor • shipwrecked on a desert island with gin and tonic on tap • hotel manager • tramp • vicar • model • singer • hotelier and ski instructor in the Alps • drummer in a big band • fireman • hovercraft pilot • psychiatrist • political organizer • world traveller • beachcomber • Prime Minister • lock-keeper • cab driver • manager of an opera company • truck driver • midwife • marriage bureau counsellor • electrical works engineer • barmaid • housewife with pay.

11

Obstacles to the development of creativity

The constraints on staff discussed in the previous chapter almost certainly have a substantial knock-on effect on pupils and students. This chapter explores other features of school and college life which teachers regard as inhibiting to their students' creativity. These are summarized in Tables 11.1 and 11.2.

ATTITUDES AND BEHAVIOUR OF OTHER PEOPLE

Almost a third of the staff interviewed regard inappropriate adult attitudes and expectations as counter-productive to creativity. One female primary teacher felt strongly that adults imposing their standards on children is one of the biggest hindrances. The assumption that children can do something better if they've 'taken it seriously' and 'put in something of themselves' can stifle their creative efforts, she believes.

A further education lecturer, very successful in raising the academic performance and personal self-esteem of young people previously regarded as failures, provides a graphic account of the stultifying effect of inappropriate adult interference:

Table 11.1 The six factors which Project 1000 teachers think most hinder the development of creativity (N = 972)

Characteristic	% of teachers who think it hinders
Constrained environment	83
Home where child's activities mostly prescribed	73
Encouraging quick work	66
Assessment by examination	61
Peer group pressure	53
Stressing differences between work and play	39

Source: Adapted from Fryer, 1989.

Quite often I see a child being creative with Lego, using his imagination, and a parent says 'What are you doing? How about doing this? Don't you think

Table 11.2 Factors the teachers who were interviewed think would inhibit in the development of creativity (N = 31)

Factor	%
Affective/personality	
pupils' fear of mistakes, teachers' fear of admitting ignorance, classroom control through fear, peer pressure, inappropriate adult attitudes, anxiety breeding practices – competitive or restrictive, constant criticism, excessively high or inappropriate expectations, insular or rigid attitudes, lack of interest or understanding.	58.0
Cognitive/task factors	
extremely didactic approach, assumption that there is only one right way to do this thing, formal syllabus, examinations.	25.8
Environmental factors	
poor physical environment, lack of resources, too much television or video viewing out of school, time constraints, excessive obsession with tidiness on part of school, unnecessary rules.	29.0

Source: Adapted from Fryer, 1989.

you ought to have some headlights?'. Now this could be a nice idea – appropriate at some point. But if the child is absorbed in something and the parent interferes, then the child may lose interest and move on to something else.

I've always thought we should have a session with parents on when to intervene and when to stand back. Sometimes children need their imaginations firing, but once this is operating, adults should stand back and let them take over.

Here's another example. Is the end-product always the child's work? Yes, we are there to spark off ideas, but are we there to direct the pen or whatever? . . . . 'You must put two ears on the rabbit, because rabbits have ears and you must put whiskers, because rabbits have whiskers'. I don't see that as our role. Yes, we are there to promote learning, but if they haven't realized where the eyes go, then that's the stage they're at.

They will develop through discussion and they will start thinking about things or looking at pictures, but if the child is just at the stage of messing around with glue and putting things on paper . . . . I think we should be aware of the child's level of development before we interfere too much. Otherwise, we can impose our values in a way which prevents children from getting anything out of the learning experience.

At school, I've seen some very good teachers who bring out the best in children and others where children have to be so precise, they get bored and fed up. Or teachers over-direct, 'You don't do things like that. Cut it out straight. Let's put it on the wall. John, you put that there. Sarah, you put that there'. So there's nothing of the children left in the end-product. They've been too guided in the way that they've done it. Other staff encourage. They praise and negotiate how children might display their work, but not by putting a child down . . . .

I'm not saying that children don't have to learn how to do things correctly, but they can learn from mistakes, can't they? It's like early science with colours. If you give children yellow and blue paint and stand back and watch, it's much more magical for them to make discoveries, than saying 'Come on. Mix yellow with blue to get green'.

A female reception teacher thought the following to be counter-productive:

being too traditional and formal in your teaching methods. You've got to be relaxed about it. I've stopped feeling guilty when I don't stick to my plan and, instead, follow up something which has cropped up, because [I have found that] the children have gained from it and enjoyed this learning [experience].

THE SCHOOL ETHOS

A high school teacher described two different conditions, both of which she believes are unhelpful to creative education:

In many ways this school is too laid back. There's a very nice, friendly atmosphere but I don't think the children feel a sense of school identity . . . children don't talk about the achievements of other pupils. It's not positive enough. It's so liberal that it's not encouraging. You have to put some boundaries, don't you? You can be so permissive that you're actually destroying things in the children, because you're creating frustration. If the boundaries are too elastic, children are constantly pushing against them, not knowing where it's going to end . . . .

My children went to a very restrictive, small grammar school. The atmosphere was very competitive and standards were high. The children knew what was expected of them. My son, who had always been good at art and had a fantastic imagination right from being a toddler, failed O-level art. Yet he had been the most creative of all our children. At this school he was constantly being told that his work was not up to standard. It killed his joy in art. Here was a very creative child restricted by that atmosphere.

We noticed a difference when he moved to another grammar school which also had very high standards and was very successful, but it had a far more . . . encouraging atmosphere. He went on to get A-level art there.

The latter school appears to have achieved a balance conducive to learning.

OUT-OF-SCHOOL ACTIVITIES

There is also a concern among teachers that some children are missing valuable play experiences out of school, for example:

As a teacher of English and drama for the past thirteen years, I've noticed that many children find it difficult to be original. They lack imagination in writing and drama work. I am convinced that the onset of the technological age is having a serious effect on the development of children's imagination. Ideas and thoughts from TV, videos and computers are often duplicated in their work. Lots of children seem to be missing out on that important 'let's pretend' stage.

(high school head of drama)

This same concern was echoed by other staff, for instance:

Out of school, children who watch TV and video and play computer games more than they read will show less creativity, less original thought and less imagination than the child who plays or reads – and this is transferred to the school situation. To cope with this, I try to encourage children to spend more time reading or involving themselves in more active pursuits. I persuade parents to play a more active role in regulating how much video and computer time children have. I think there is some creativity involved in computing apart from the games, such as in programming. I also think some parents will regulate TV and some will want to, but won't have the ability.

(Merseyside English teacher)

These teachers' concerns echo those of Mock (1970), but not everyone agrees about the negative effects of new technology. It is not technology *per se* which is de-skilling, according to an inventive electronics lecturer, but rather the fact that people do not always realize its potential.

Indeed, computers can give children the opportunity to try out alternative scenarios, to ask 'What would happen if?', to explore the consequences of risk-taking in total safety (Tisone and Wismar, 1985).

INAPPROPRIATE ASSESSMENT

Over-zealous correcting of pupils' work can be counter-productive too. As a primary teacher commented 'I try to tell children that getting something wrong is a way of learning. If a child gets a cross on his or her book, it's like a statement of failure. Constantly telling children their writing is untidy is inhibiting'. Handwriting is a particularly difficult problem for left-handers. Discrimination against left-handed people is not normally acknowledged. However, being left-handed in a world designed mainly for right-handers does make one acutely aware of alternative perspectives – which can be quite a fertile source of creative ideas. Might this provide an alternative explanation for the preoccupation of left-handers with creativity?

Formally assessing everything can inhibit children. One teacher recounted that some children felt they were unable to make a mark on the paper because of distressing past experiences of assessment. In the interests of creative learning, Torrance (1965, p. 148) makes the same point: 'children need periods during which they can experiment, make mistakes, and test various approaches without fear of evaluation and the failure that making a mistake implies'. In his experience, children are monitored so much that they hardly dare make a leap in their thinking for fear of criticism. This forces them to take the safest option, avoiding experimentation and never learning how to find and correct their mistakes.

A geography specialist described how insensitive marking encourages children to 'play safe', writing only what they know to be correct. She finds that this results in their producing mostly bland and unimaginative work. Renfrow (1984) shares this view and maintains that an excessive emphasis on accuracy is counter-productive since it discourages risk-taking, experimentation and estimating on the part of pupils. In similar vein, Cropley argues that 'Courageous mistakes often promote better understanding of basic principles than pedestrian correctness, and learning is frequently fostered as effectively by an incorrect answer as a correct one' and he emphasizes how useful it is to realize that there is more than one way of being right (Cropley, 1967, p. 92).

Teachers are really concerned that the new testing procedures will undermine children's self-confidence. As one teacher put it 'What do you do if a child fails at seven, again at eleven and so on?'. A deputy head described how he has worked hard to build children's confidence, which could be completely undone by an excessive emphasis on testing. Broadfoot *et al.* (1993) have reached the same conclusion. They point out that British teachers may soon be in the same position as their French counterparts, who have to spend a lot of time building the self-concepts of children who have failed repeatedly. Clearly this is something which needs to be addressed.

THE CURRICULUM

According to Perkin (1995), an experienced teacher and lecturer who has conducted school inspections in Britain, it is possible to deliver the UK's national curriculum in a way which addresses the development of pupils' creativity. He believes this to be the case, even though the curriculum may look daunting and teachers feel pressured.

He points out that, for the first time ever, problem solving is required in science, design technology and mathematics. The process of learning is given more emphasis than previously. In art, children are encouraged to appreciate the work of great artists, as a stimulus, a jumping off point, for their own creative work. This sounds rather more positive than the experience of Amabile (1983) who describes how, as a young child, she was expected to 'copy' the great masters, using a set of wax crayons!

Perkin is himself an inspiring and enthusiastic educator. In his experience, examples of good practice include those where innovative teachers build formal assessment into their teaching. So the assessment itself becomes a formative and positive experience for the pupils.

Torrance (1984) argues that it could be counter-productive to bring every child to the same level of achievement in all subjects. It is probably the dream of most teachers that every child might excel in some of them. The following fable illustrates what can happen if, instead, we select well-roundedness as the goal.

The Animal School by G. H. Reavis
(Included with the kind permission of the American Association of School Administrators © 1949)

Once upon a time the animals decided they must do something heroic to meet the problems of 'a new world'. So they organized a school.

They adopted an activity curriculum consisting of running, climbing, swimming, and flying. To make it easier to administer the curriculum, *all* the animals took *all* the subjects.

The duck was excellent in swimming, in fact, better than his instructor; but he made only passing grades in flying and was very poor in running. Since he was slow in running he had to stay after school and also drop swimming in order to practise running. This was kept up until his web feet were badly worn and he was only average in swimming. *But average was acceptable in school, so nobody worried about that except the duck.*

The rabbit started at the top of the class in running, but had a nervous break-down because of so much make-up work in swimming.

The squirrel was excellent in climbing until he developed frustration in the flying class when his teacher made him start from the ground up instead of from tree-top down. He also developed 'charley horses' from over-exertion and then got C in climbing and D in running. The eagle was a problem child and was disciplined severely. In the climbing class he beat all the others to the top of the tree, but insisted on using his own way to get there.

At the end of the year, an abnormal eel that could swim exceedingly well, and also run, climb, and fly a little, had the highest average and was valedictorian. The prairie dogs stayed out of school and fought the tax levy because the administration would not add digging and burrowing to the curriculum. They apprenticed their child to a badger and later joined the groundhogs and gophers to start a successful private school.

Does this fable have a moral?

SUMMARY

Obviously any constraints which seriously affect the performance of staff will influence their pupils' performance. Some teachers expressed considerable concern that children are either missing out on imaginary play or are excessively influenced by the media in a way that dampens their creative learning. Many of the things which the Project 1000 teachers think inhibit young people's creativity revolve around adults, in particular their relationship with and attitudes towards the young people. These include excessive intrusiveness when children are absorbed in their learning, inappropriate adult attitudes and insensitive assessment. There is also the view that extreme inflexibility and excessive permissiveness are equally counter-productive.

12

Creative teaching and learning
for the future

TEACHERS, LECTURERS AND CREATIVITY

Many of the teachers and lecturers who took part in Project 1000 have every reason for regarding themselves as creative. Yet, on the whole, they tend not to see themselves in this way. This is strange given the ingenuity staff display in capturing children's enthusiasm, getting around unhelpful systems and coping with significant pressure. What is clear is that there is an enormous pool of talent and a wealth of experience which merits being well-resourced.

As would be expected from a broadly-based and varied sample, staff have shown differing degrees of interest in creativity and, as a group, they have identified a whole range of factors they regard as supportive of creativity development. Informative detailed accounts have been provided by individual staff. Many are keen to know more about the whole area of creativity, especially what other teachers think about it.

WHY TEACH FOR CREATIVITY?

Land and Jarman (1992) suggest that we have reached a *breakpoint*. Many aspects of our lives will never be the same again. But, as they describe, such points of transformation are inevitable and natural, even though they seem uncontrollable and the future hard to predict.

We all react differently to change. It may be embraced, tolerated or resisted. In the UK, response to significant change is predictably paradoxical. On the one hand, the introduction of new technology is generally being welcomed. There is increasing interest in updating via a range of innovation initiatives. At the same time, there is evidence of a stepping back in the form of a *back to basics* movement. Land and Jarman (1992, p. 63) describe their experience of this phenomenon in the United States:

This Back to Basics mentality is fully operational today in countless organizations from government to education to religious groups. The report of a distinguished panel of American educators entitled, *A Nation at Risk*, suggested a Back to Basics solution for America's educational crisis. The outcome today is classic. The initial response was to require tougher graduation requirements for high school students, eliminate so-called frills from the curriculum, and impose more stringent testing. Over the short-term improvements were seen, but very quickly the dropout rate increased, test scores plummeted, and the prospect of a long-term decline in public education still looms.

Sturner (1987, p. 38) describes how too little change can lead to 'suffocation', whilst too much results in 'fragmentation'. He maintains that the optimum goal is midway between these two extremes.

In times of great stability, creative teaching and learning serves to drive people out of stagnation in the direction of progress. When rapid change is the norm, there is the danger of simply being swept along. Then, creativity is required to make sense of what is happening, to cope with novel conditions and to achieve a new equilibrium somewhere between chaos and stagnation.

TAKING CREATIVITY DEVELOPMENT SERIOUSLY

A number of successful organizations are taking the development of creative skills very seriously. This is enabling them to move away from old markets, inflexible hierarchies and clogging bureaucracy towards less complicated, flatter structures, more able to respond to new demands and opportunities. It is likely that educational systems will also have to respond to the new conditions. Some progress has been made, but there is still a long way to go.

As Storr (1988) has pointed out, it is our creative skills which enable us to flexibly adapt to change in every area of our lives. So it is particularly odd that this capacity is largely ignored in school and college education. At present, education for creativity is almost exclusively available to the few.

It has been suggested that one reason for this is a deep-seated mistrust of imagination, which Kearney (1988) and Egan (1992) have traced back to the Ancient World and beyond. It now seems appropriate to shake off archaic notions of creativity, including inspiration and incubation, in favour of more up-to-date explanations. It is also time to abandon terminology which underplays the pervasive role of imagination in thinking and concept formation (see Chapter 4; Johnson-Laird, 1987; 1988; Paul, 1993). Despite the strong association between the arts and imagination, the arts tend to be undervalued in education, as quite a few of the teachers have recounted.

AVOIDING BANDWAGONS

All too often the results of careful and complex research have been translated into simplistic notions, which have then been pounced upon to create educational bandwagons. As Cropley (1992) warns, excessive enthusiasm combined with ill-thought out and hasty policy will be counter-productive. We have already experienced this with creativity development in the UK in the 1960s, when complex recommendations were largely ignored or translated into simplistic practices (as recounted by 'Lesley' in Chapter 7). As we have seen from the teachers' contributions, creativity is complex. Teaching for creative outcomes needs to address that complexity.

CREATIVE WORK

Not all products and ideas which deserve the accolade 'perfect' or 'excellent' can legitimately be described as creative. Creative work is work which pushes forward the boundaries in ways which are appropriate, useful, valuable and so on. As discussed in Chapter 2, there are quite stringent objective criteria for creative products and ideas, although the very nature of creativity means that there will always be an element of subjectivity in any evaluation.

Young people can gain valuable transferable skills devising their own criteria and using them to assess their own work, as described by the design staff. Clearly, when this is a group activity, it needs to be handled sensitively.

It has been pointed out that there is no evidence to suggest that really creative people are qualitatively different. Many characteristics indicative of creativity have been cited, of which perhaps the most pervasive is a high level of motivation, which shows up as persistence, tenacity and commitment.

SURPRISING FINDINGS

Although the teachers have provided many valuable insights and useful suggestions, it was rather surprising to find that so many of them hold some old-fashioned views about creativity. It was even more unexpected to find that different groups of teachers see creativity differently. This was especially true of male and female staff. It was also interesting to find that their views about creativity co-vary with their views about teaching, how they see pupils and how they feel about them. In effect, their views about creativity appear indicative of some kind of underlying value system linked to person orientation (see Chapter 5).

TEACHER TRAINING

It was not so unexpected to find that where teachers recalled the development of creativity being addressed in their training, this related mainly to the arts, since this is how creativity is popularly perceived. But clearly there is a need to address the development of creativity in the training of science and business studies teachers and lecturers. Certainly, quite a number of Project 1000 staff are aware of the relevance of creative education to the whole curriculum.

Indeed, there is a need for all trainee teachers to be more informed about creativity in order to clear up misconceptions about notions of giftedness and the relationship between creativity and intelligence. Information about the educational programmes and materials available would assist them.

TEACHING FOR CREATIVITY

Armed with the necessary knowledge and skills, it seems highly likely that children will become more skilled in being creative by working at tasks which require creative solutions. Allowing a certain amount of choice in the curriculum, which many staff recommend, does give children the opportunity to take responsibility for and a pride in their work.

The results of Project 1000 have demonstrated that the teachers are, on the whole, very aware of the background factors which support creativity and some of them are already actively implementing these, or would like to do so. However, hardly any of them know much about teaching creative problem solving (see Chapter 9). There is evidence to suggest that the kinds of training programmes and techniques highlighted in this book can help young people to become better at devising creative solutions. It has been suggested that the function these programmes serve can be explained psychologically, without resorting to archaic or mysterious explanations.

It is unfortunate that teachers' efforts to support their students' creativity are frequently dogged by resource constraints. At the same time there is some evidence of progress, with the inclusion of *some* problem solving in the UK national curriculum, as well as renewed public interest in education and in creativity and innovation.

To prepare for the future, children and young adults need a good range of problem solving, communication and practical skills and opportunities to try these out confidently. They need skills for accessing information, as well as experience in reasoning by analogy. Learning activities which encourage them to imagine are essential, as are those in which they can get really absorbed. Teachers who are really keen to develop creativity prefer to teach in a whole variety of ways and value every child's contribution.

The teachers who took part in this study have contributed a great deal to our understanding. As we have seen, creativity is a complex concept. It has many facets. Education for creativity needs to be designed to address them all. This demands high levels of skill, insight, sensitivity and vision on the part of teachers, as well as proper support for the valuable work they do.

References

Amabile, T. M. (1982) Social psychology of creativity: a consensual assessment technique, *Journal of Personality and Social Psychology*, 43, pp. 997–1013.

Amabile, T. M. (1983) *The Social Psychology of Creativity*, Springer-Verlag, New York, NY.

Ausubel, D. P. (1978) The nature and measurement of creativity, *Psychologia: an International Journal of Psychology in the Orient*, Vol. 21, no. 4, pp. 179–91.

Ayman, I. (1993) Dialogues of transitions to a global society. Paper given at the Presidents' Convocation, Creative Education Foundation, Buffalo, NY.

Barber, M. (1994) *Young People and their Attitudes to School: an interim report of a research project in the Centre for Successful Schools*, Keele University.

Besemer, S. P. and Treffinger, D. J. (1981) Analysis of creative products: review and synthesis, *The Journal of Creative Behavior*, Vol. 15, no. 3, pp. 158–77.

Best, D. (1982) Can creativity be taught? *British Journal of Educational Studies*, Vol. 30, no. 3, pp. 280–94.

Bjerstedt, A. (1976) Explorations in creativity, *Didakometry and Sociometry*, Vol. 8, no. 2, pp. 3–19.

British Psychological Society (1986) Achievement in the Primary School: a Statement for a House of Commons Committee, *Bulletin*, The British Psychological Society, April, pp. 121–5.

Broadfoot, P., Osborn, M., Gilly, M. and Bûcher, A. (1993) *Perceptions of Teaching: Primary School Teachers in England and France*, Cassell, London.

Bruner, J. S. (1962) The creative surprise, in H. E. Gruber, G. Terrell and M. Wortheimer (eds.) *Contemporary Approaches to Creative Thinking*, Atherton Press, New York, NY.

Bruner, J. S. (1966) The will to learn, in J. M. Whitehead (ed.) (1975) *Personality and Learning*, Vol. 1, Hodder & Stoughton & Open University, London.

Bryant, P. E. and Trabasso, T. (1971) Transitive inferences and memory in young children, *Nature*, no. 232, pp. 456–8.

Chase, W. G. and Simon, H. A. (1973) Perception in chess, *Cognitive Psychology*, 4, pp. 55–81.

Chi, M., Feltovich, P. J. and Glaser, R. (1981) Categorization and representation of physics problems by experts and novices, *Cognitive Science*, 5, pp. 121–5.

Cohen, G., Eysenck, M. W. and LeVoi, M. E. (1986) *Memory: A Cognitive Approach*, Open University Press, Milton Keynes.

Collings, J. A. (1978) A psychological study of female science specialists in the sixth form. Unpublished PhD thesis, University of Bradford.

Collings, J. and Smithers, A. (1984) Person orientation and science choice, *European Journal of Science Education*, Vol. 6, no. 1, pp. 55–65.

Craik, F. I. M., and Lockhart, R. S. (1972) Levels of processing: a framework for memory research, *Journal of Verbal Learning and Verbal Behavior*, 11, pp. 671–84.

Crawford, R. P. (1978) The techniques of creative thinking, in G. A. Davis and J. A. Scott (eds.) *Training Creative Thinking*, Krieger, Huntington, NY.

Cropley, A. J. (1967) *Creativity*, Longman, London.

Cropley, A. J. (1992) *More Than One Way of Fostering Creativity*, Ablex, Norwood, NJ.

Davis, G. A. (1983) *Creativity is Forever*, Kendall/Hunt, Iowa.

De Bono, E. (1993) *Teach Your Child How To Think*, Penguin, Harmondsworth.

DeGroot, A. (1966) Perception and memory versus thought: some old ideas and recent findings, in B. Kleinmuntz (ed.) *Problem Solving Research, Method and Theory*, Wiley, New York, NY.

Donaldson, M. (1978) *Children's Minds*, Wm Collins, Glasgow.

Donaldson, M. (1982) Conservation: what is the question? *British Journal of Psychology*, 73, pp. 199–207.

Eberle, R. F. (1966) *Teaching for creative-productive thinking through subject matter content*, Edwardsville Community Schools, Edwardsville, Ill.

Egan, K. (1992) *Imagination in Teaching and Learning*, Routledge, London.

Entwistle, N. (1982) Approaches and styles: recent research on students' learning, *Educational Analysis*, Vol. 4, no. 2, pp. 43–54.

Entwistle, N. (1987) *SSRC regional seminar on the PhD*, Sheffield University.

Eriksson, A. (1970) *Pedagogisk-psykologiska problem-lararenkater om kreativitet I skolan*, Malmö University Press (selective English translation by Inga Betts).

Fabun, D. (1968) *You and Creativity*, Macmillan, New York, NY.

Fryer, B. (1994) Mentoring experience, in B. Little (ed.) *Supporting Learning in the Workplace, Proceedings of the Joint National Conference of the Open University and Leeds Metropolitan University*, Leeds, 19–20 September.

Fryer, M. (1989) Teachers' Views on Creativity. Unpublished PhD thesis, Leeds Metropolitan University, Leeds.

Fryer, M. (1993) Facilitators of creativity. Paper given at the 39th Creative Problem Solving Institute of the Creative Education Foundation, Buffalo, NY.

Fryer, M. (1994a) The primacy of creative problem solving: a review of thinking, learning, problem solving and imagination. Paper given at the 40th Creative Problem Solving Institute of the Creative Education Foundation, Buffalo, NY.

Fryer, M. (1994b) Management style and views about creativity, in H. Geschka, S. Moger and T. Rickards (eds.) *Creativity and Innovation: The Power of Synergy*, Geschka & Partner Unternehmensberatung, Darmstadt, Germany.

Fryer, M. and Collings, J. A. (1991a) Teachers' views about creativity, *British Journal of Educational Psychology*, 61, pp. 207–19.

Fryer, M. and Collings, J. A. (1991b) British teachers' views of creativity, *The Journal of Creative Behavior*, Vol. 25, no. 1, pp. 75–81.

Gardner, H. (1993) *Multiple Intelligences: The Theory in Practice*, Basic Books, New York, NY.

Gellerman. S. (1979) Personnel and productivity, *Management Today*, 142, pp. 82–5.

Geschka, H. (1994) Visual confrontation – developing ideas from pictures, in H. Geschka, S. Moger and T. Rickards (eds.) *Creativity and Innovation: The Power of Synergy*, Geschka & Partner Unternehmensberatung, Darmstadt, Germany.

Getzels, J. W. and Jackson, P. (1962) *Creativity and Intelligence*, Wiley, New York, NY.

Glasser, W. (1992) *The Quality School*, Harper Perennial, New York, NY.

Glasser, W. (1993) *The Quality School Teacher*, Harper Perennial, New York, NY.

Gilhooly, K. J. (1982) *Thinking: Directed, Undirected and Creative*, Academic Press, London.

Gordon, W. J. J. (1961) *Synectics*, Harper & Row, New York, NY.

Goswami, U. (1992) *Analogical Reasoning in Children: Essays in Developmental Psychology*, Erlbaum, Hove.

Gray and Satterly (1981) Formal or informal? a reassessment of the British evidence, *British Journal of Educational Psychology*, Vol. 51, no. 2, pp. 187–96.

Greenhalgh, L. (1985) Effects of sex-role differences on approach to interpersonal and interorganizational negotiations. Private paper in Helgesen, S. op. cit.

Guilford, J. P. (1950) Creativity, *American Psychologist*, 5, pp. 444–54.

Guilford, J. P. (1977) *Way Beyond the IQ*, The Creative Education Foundation Inc., in association with Bearly, Buffalo, NY.

Helgesen, S. (1990) *The Female Advantage: Women's Ways of Leadership*, Doubleday, New York, NY.

Hocevar, D. (1981) Measurement of creativity: review and critique, *Journal of Personality Assessment*, Vol. 45, no. 5, pp. 450–64.

Holloway, C. (1978) *Cognitive Psychology: Learning and Instruction*, Open University, Milton Keynes.

Hudson, L. (1966) *Contrary Imaginations*, Methuen, London.

Jackson, P. W. and Messick, S. (1965) The person, the product and the response: conceptual problems in the assessment of creativity, *Journal of Personality*, 33, pp. 1–19.

Jerome, J. K. (1993) *Three Men in a Boat*, Wordsworth Editions, Ware, Hertfordshire.

Johnson-Laird, P. N. (1983) *Mental Models*, Cambridge University Press.

Johnson-Laird, P. N. (1987) Reasoning, imagining and creating, *Bulletin of the British Psychological Society*, 40, pp. 121–29.

Johnson-Laird, P. N. (1988) *The Computer and the Mind*, Harvard University Press.

Kearney, R. (1988) *The Wake of Imagination*, Hutchinson, London.

Kneller, G. F. (1965) *The Art and Science of Creativity*, Holt, Rinehart & Winston, New York, NY.

Kuhn, T. S. (1970) *The Structure of Scientific Revolutions*, University of Chicago Press.

Land, G. T. L. (1973) *Grow or Die: The Unifying Principle of Transformation*, Dell Publishing Co. Inc., New York, NY.

Land, G. T. L. and Jarman, B. (1992) *Breakpoint and Beyond*, HarperBusiness, USA.

Le Corbusier (1946) *Towards a New Architecture*, The Architectural Press, London.

Lesgold, A. *et al.* (1988) Expertise in a complex skill: diagnosing X-ray pictures, in M. T. H. Chi, R. Glaser and M. J. Farr (eds.) *The Nature of Expertise*, Erlbaum, Hillsdale, NJ.

Lucas, P. G. (1963) *Man's Search for Reality*, Odhams, Watford.

MacKinnon, D. W. (1962) The personality correlates of creativity: a study of American architects, in G. S. Neilsen (ed.) *Proceedings of the Fourteenth Congress on Applied Psychology*, 2, Munksgaard, pp. 11–39.

Maslow, A. H. (1954) *Motivation and Personality*, Harper & Row, New York, NY.

McClelland, D. C. (1963) The calculated risk: an aspect of scientific performance, in C. W. Taylor and F. Barron (eds.) *Scientific Creativity: Its Recognition and Development*, Wiley, New York, NY.

McGregor, D. (1960) *The Human Side of Enterprise*, McGraw-Hill, New York, NY.

McVicker Hunt, J. (1960) Experience and the development of motivation: some re-interpretations, *Child Development*, 31, pp. 489–504.

Mead, M. (1962) Male and female, in J. Oates (ed.) (1979) *Early Cognitive Development*, Croom Helm & Open University, London.

Mednick, S. A. (1962) The associative basis of the creative process, *Psychological Review*, 69, pp. 220–32.

Merritt, S. (1994) Ins and Outs of Imagery, in H. Geschka, S. Moger and T. Rickards (eds.) *Creativity and Innovation: The Power of Synergy*, Geschka & Partner Unternehmensberatung, Darmstadt, Germany.

Mitchell, E. (1993) Paradigms for transformation to a meaningful global future. Address to the 1993 Presidents' Convocation, Creative Education Foundation, Buffalo, NY.

Mock, R. (1970) *Education and the Imagination*, Chatto and Windus, London.

Motamedi, K. (1982) Extending the concept of creativity, The Journal of Creative Behavior, Vol. 16, no. 2, pp. 75–89.

Murray, H. G. and Denny, J. P. (1969) Interaction of ability level and interpolated activity in human problem solving, *Psychological Reports*, 24, pp. 271–6.

Nias, J. (1989) *Primary Teachers Talking: A Study of Teaching as Work*, Routledge, London.

Ochse, R. E. (1990) *Before the Gates of Excellence: the Determinants of Creative Genius*, Cambridge University Press.

Ogilvie, E. (1974) Creativity and curriculum structure, *Educational Research*, 16, pp. 126–32.

Ohuche, N. M. (1986) The ideal pupil as perceived by Nigerian (Igbo) teachers and Torrance's creative personality, *International Review of Education*, Vol. 32, no. 8, pp. 191–6.

Olton, R. M. (1979) Experimental studies of incubation: searching for the elusive, *The Journal of Creative Behavior*, 13, pp. 9–22.

Oppenheim, A. N. (1966) *Questionnaire Design and Attitude Measurement*, Heinemann, London.

Osborn, A. F. (1993) *Applied Imagination*, Creative Education Foundation Press, Buffalo, NY.

Parnes, S. J. (1985) *A Facilitating Kind of Leadership*, Bearly, Buffalo, NY.

Parnes, S. J. (1992a) *Source Book for Creative Problem Solving*, Creative Education Foundation Press, Buffalo, NY.

Parnes, S. J. (1992b) *Visionizing*, Creative Education Foundation Press, Buffalo, NY.

Pask, G. (1976) Styles and strategies of learning, *British Journal of Educational Psychology*, 46, pp. 128–48.

Pask, G. and Scott, B. C. E. (1972) Learning strategies and individual competence, *International Journal of Man-Machine Studies*, 4, pp. 217–53.

Paul, R. W. (1993) The Logic of Creative and Critical Thinking, *American Behavioral Scientist*, Vol. 37, no. 1, pp. 21–39, Sage, Thousand Oaks.

Perkin, R. (1995) Personal communication.

Perkins, D. N. (1981) *The Mind's Best Work*, Harvard University Press.

Popescu-Nevianu, P. and Cretsu, T. (1986) Study of teachers' creative abilities, *Revue Roumaine des Sciences Sociales*, Vol. 30, no. 2, pp. 129–34 (selective English translation by Ludmilla Lewis).

Razik, T. A. (1967) Psychometric measurement of creativity, in R. Mooney, and T. A. Razik (eds.) *Explorations in Creativity*, Harper & Row, New York, NY.

Renfrow, M. J. (1984) The truth in error, *The Journal of Creative Behavior*, Vol. 18, no. 4, pp. 227–36.

Roe, A. (1952) A psychological study of eminent psychologists and anthropologists and a comparison with biological and physical scientists, *Psychological Monographs*, no. 67.

Roe, A. (1963) Psychological approaches to creativity in science, in M. A. Coler (ed.) *Essays on Creativity in the Sciences*, New York University Press.

Rogers, C. R. (1954) Towards a theory of creativity, in P. E. Vernon (ed.) (1970) *Creativity*, Penguin, Harmondsworth.

Rogers, C. R. (1983) *Freedom to Learn for the 80s*, Charles E. Merrill, Columbus, Ohio.

Roth, I. (1978) *Cognitive Psychology: Perception (Part 1)*, Open University, Milton Keynes.

Shallcross, D. J. (1985) *Teaching Creative Behavior*, Bearly, Buffalo, NY.

Schaefer, C. (1973) An exploratory study of teachers' descriptions of the ideal pupil, *Psychology in Schools*, Vol. 10, no. 4, pp. 444–7.

Shekerjian, D. (1991) *Uncommon Genius: How Great Ideas are Born*, Penguin, Harmondsworth.

Simon, H. A. (1966) Scientific discovery and the psychology of problem solving, in R. G. Colodny (ed.) *Mind and Cosmos: Essays in Contemporary Science and Philosophy*, Pittsburgh University Press.

Staniszewski, M. A. (1995) *Believing is Seeing: Creating the Culture of Art*, Penguin, Harmondsworth.

Stein, M. I. (1981) Nurturing creative-and-all-other children: introducing the concept of contricipation. Keynote address to Creativefest '81, Fourth Annual State Conference on Education of the Gifted and Talented, sponsored by Rutgers University.

Stein, M. I. (1983) Creativity in genesis, *The Journal of Creative Behavior*, Vol. 17, no. 1, pp. 1–8.

Stein, M. I. (1984) *Making the Point*, The Mews Press, Amagansett, NY.

Stein, M. I. (1993) Personal communication.

Stein, M. I. (1994a) *Stimulating Creativity, Vol. 1, Individual Procedures*, The Mews Press, Amagansett, NY.

Stein, M. I. (1994b) *Stimulating Creativity, Vol. 2, Group Procedures*, The Mews Press, Amagansett, NY.

Stein, M. I. (1994c) *Gifted, Talented, and Creative Young People: A Guide to Theory, Teaching, and Research*, The Mews Press, Amagansett, NY.

Sternberg, R. J. (ed.) (1988) *The Nature of Creativity: Contemporary Psychological Perspectives*, Cambridge University Press.

Storr, A. (1988) *The School of Genius*, Andre Deutsch, London.

Sturner, W. F. (1987) *Risking Change: Endings and Beginnings*, Bearly, Buffalo, NY.

Times Educational Supplement, *With love and rigour*, 4 October, p. 23, 1985.

Tisone, J. M. and Wismar, B. L. (1985) Microcomputers: how can they be used to enhance creative development? *The Journal of Creative Behavior*, Vol. 19, no. 2, pp. 97–103.

Torrance, E. P. (1962) *Guiding Creative Talent*, Prentice-Hall, Englewood Cliffs, New Jersey.

Torrance, E. P. (1965) *Rewarding Creative Behavior*, Prentice-Hall, Englewood Cliffs, New Jersey.

Torrance, E. P. (1967) Nurture of Creative Talents, *Theory into Practice*, 5, pp. 168–73, 201–2.

Torrance, E. P. (1974) *Torrance Tests of Creative Thinking*, Ginn & Company (Xerox Corporation), Lexington, M.A.

Torrance, E. P. (1975) Preliminary Manual: Ideal Child Checklist, *Georgia Studies of Creative Behavior*, Athens, Georgia.

Torrance, E. P. (1984) *Mentor Relationships: How they Aid Creative Achievement, Endure, Change, and Die*, Bearly, Buffalo, NY.

Torrance, E. P. (1988) The nature of creativity as manifest in testing, in R. J. Sternberg (ed.) op. cit.

Torrance, E. P. and Myers, R. E. (1970) *Creative Learning and Teaching*, Harper & Row, New York, NY.

Tyndall, J. (1868) *Faraday as a Discoverer*, Longmans, Green, London.

VanGundy, A. B. (1984) *Managing Group Creativity: A Modular Approach to Problem Solving*, Amacom, New York, NY.

VanGundy, A. B. (1988) *Techniques of Structured Problem Solving*, (2nd edn), Van Nostrand Reinhold, New York, NY.

VanGundy, A. B. (1992) *Idea Power: Techniques and Resources to Unleash the Creativity in your Organization*, Amacom, New York, NY.

Von Oech, R. (1990) *A Whack on the Side of the Head*, Warner Books, New York, NY.

Wallas, G. (1926) The art of thought, in P. E. Vernon (ed.) (1970) *Creativity*, Penguin, Harmondsworth.

Warnock, M. (1976) *Imagination*, Faber & Faber, London.

Wason, P. C. (1978) *Cognitive Psychology: Learning and Problem Solving* (Part 2), Open University, Milton Keynes.

Webberley, R. and Litt, L. (1976), *Personality and Learning: Intelligence and Creativity*, Open University, Milton Keynes.

Weisberg, R. W. (1986) *Creativity: Genius and Other Myths*, Freeman, New York, NY.

Weisberg, R. W. (1993) *Creativity: Beyond the Myth of Genius*, Freeman, New York, NY.

Weisberg, R. W. and Springer, K. J. (1961) Environmental factors in creative function, *Arch. gen. Psychiat*, 5, pp. 554–64.

Wheeler-Brownlee, G. (1985) Imagination: the connection enigma, *The Journal of Creative Behavior*, Vol. 19, no. 4, pp. 255–69.

White, A. (1990) *The Language of Imagination*, Blackwell, Oxford.

Williams, F. E. (1964) Reinforcement of originality, in *Reinforcement in Classroom Learning*, Washington: U.S. Dept. of Health, Education and Welfare.

Woodworth, R. S. and Schlosberg, H. (1954) *Experimental Psychology*, (3rd edn), Methuen, London.

Young, J. G. (1982) Negative spaces, *The Journal of Creative Behavior*, Vol. 16, no. 4, pp. 256–64.

Young, R. E. (1984) Teaching equals indoctrination: the dominant epistemic practices of our schools, *British Journal of Educational Studies*, Vol. 32, no. 3, pp. 220–38.

Index

DATE DUE

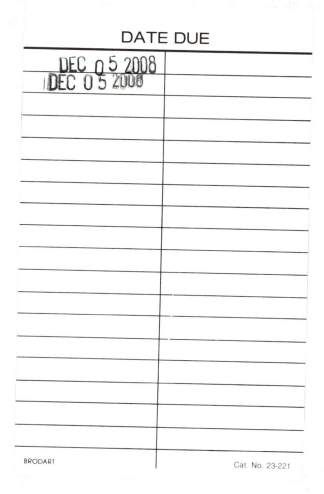

DEC 0 5 2008	
DEC 0 5 2008	

BRODART   Cat. No. 23-221